AUG 2 7 2009

GENES & DISEASE

CYSTIC FIBROSIS

GENES & DISEASE

Alzheimer's Disease

Asthma

Cystic Fibrosis

Diabetes

Down Syndrome

Hemophilia

Huntington's Disease

Parkinson's Disease

Sickle Cell Disease

Tay-Sachs Disease

GENES & DISEASE

CYSTIC FIBROSIS

Sharon Giddings, RN, BSN, MA

CHELSEA HOUSE
PUBLISHERS
An imprint of Infobase Publishing

Chelsea House
An imprint of Infobase Publishing
132 West 31st Street
New York NY 10001

Library of Congress Cataloging-in-Publication Data

Giddings, Sharon.
    Cystic fibrosis / Sharon Giddings.
       p. cm. — (Genes and disease)
    Includes bibliographical references and index.
    ISBN 978-0-7910-9694-9 (hardcover)
    1. Cystic fibrosis—Genetic aspects. 2. Cystic fibrosis. I. Title. II. Series.
    RC858.C95.G53 2009
    616.3'72—dc22   2008044771

Chelsea House books are available at special discounts when purchased in bulk quantities for businesses, associations, institutions, or sales promotions. Please call our Special Sales Department in New York at (212) 967–8800 or (800) 322–8755.

You can find Chelsea House on the World Wide Web at
http://www.chelseahouse.com

Text design by Annie O'Donnell
Cover design by Ben Peterson

Printed in the United States of America

Bang NMSG 10 9 8 7 6 5 4 3 2 1

This book is printed on acid-free paper.

All links and Web addresses were checked and verified to be correct at the time of publication. Because of the dynamic nature of the Web, some addresses and links may have changed since publication and may no longer be valid.

CONTENTS

1

WHAT IS
CYSTIC FIBROSIS?

Cystic fibrosis (CF) is an inherited, life-threatening genetic disease occurring in about 30,000 children and adults in the United States and about 70,000 people around the world. Although most CF patients are Caucasians, the disease can occur in all races and ethnic groups.

CF is caused by a flaw, or **mutation**, of a single **gene** called the **CFTR gene**—that is, the cystic fibrosis transmembrane conductance regulator gene. The damaged gene is **inherited**, or passed on, from parent to child. This mutated gene causes the body's mucous glands, which normally secrete thin, lubricating liquid (mucus), to produce thick, sticky mucus that clogs the lungs and obstructs the **pancreas**. Clogged lungs result in dangerous lung infections that often occur repeatedly throughout a patient's life. Because the pancreas produces **digestive enzymes** critical to helping the body break down and absorb food, CF patients continually experience uncomfortable and growth-threatening digestive disorders.

MORE ABOUT MUCUS

Mucous glands normally secrete liquid mucus that keeps body organs moist and lubricated. Healthy people who do not have cystic fibrosis live largely unaware of all the functions that their mucous glands carry out. The glands, located in several areas of the body, provide continuous secretion that is critical for healthy body functions. The tasks of mucus include:

◆ lubricating breathing organs to provide smooth and easy inhalation and exhalation;

◆ supporting the function of the pancreatic gland, a gland that manufactures and excretes enzymes used in normal digestion;

◆ providing for the continual, smooth passage of salt (**sodium chloride**) into and out of the epithelial **cells** that line the respiratory and gastrointestinal tracts, and the pancreatic ducts, among other body sites. The membranes encasing these cells each contain a passageway called the chloride ion channel, through which salt and water pass at regular intervals.

The damaged CFTR gene prevents function of the chloride ion channels in patients with CF, however. The normal flow of chloride ions helps control water movement in tissues. Normal water movement is needed for producing thin, free-flowing mucus. (Ultimately, it is the nonfunctioning chloride ion channels that cause the sticky, thick mucus that CF patients endure.) Thus, excessive salt accumulates in the body, where some of it eventually is excreted through the sweat glands. A patient's highly salty skin is diagnostic for CF. This sign was noted centuries ago by ancient peoples, who knew only that babies with this symptom would soon die.

Cystic fibrosis occurs in all races and ethnic groups, though much less frequently than in Caucasians (white people), in which 1 in 2,500 to 3,500 newborns have CF. In

African Americans, the disease occurs in 1 in 17,000 births. In Asian Americans, CF occurs in 1 in 31,000 newborns.

Cystic fibrosis remains incurable, and treating a patient's symptoms effectively is literally a matter of life and death. The glue-like mucus not only blocks critical life functions, some of it eventually settles deep inside the lungs. These areas provide moist, warm environments in which bacteria can flourish. The result? Serious, sometimes life-threatening, lung infections. Antibiotics are often highly effective in killing the bacteria, yet over time, new strains of these lung-based bacteria change to become resistant to these drugs. Resistance allows the altered bacterial strains to grow and flourish again in the mucus-plugged lungs and cause repeated lung infections during a patient's lifetime. Treating these infections often requires repeated episodes

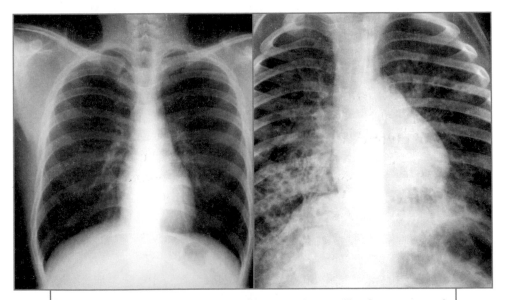

FIGURE 1.1   People with cystic fibrosis often suffer from repeated lung infections throughout their lives. This is because of the thick mucus that the mutated CFTR gene causes, which clogs lungs. Healthy lungs (*left*) do not display the same inflammation from repeated infections as the lungs of a cystic fibrosis patient (*right*).

STRESS ON A FAMILY

These off-and-on episodes spent in the hospital can significantly disrupt education, employment efforts, and family life. Families may worry about how to pay for this expensive care as they cope with daily life at home. Parents with a CF child may experience higher levels of depression than parents without a CF child. Whoever provides daily patient care can easily become overloaded with tasks such as timing prescribed therapies (medication, enzyme replacement, and/or breathing routines), preparing highly nutritional meals, and transporting the child to medical appointments. Parents' time alone together becomes limited, which may reduce the emotional support that each provides the other, and marital stress may grow as a couple copes with the sick child. If the child with CF has one or more normal siblings, these children may show behavioral problems because of a lack of parental attention and their own concerns about the health status of their sick brother or sister.

of hospitalization that occur throughout a patient's life. Eventually, infections cause permanent lung damage, including formation of scar tissue and cysts. Grave lung infection is the most common cause of death in individuals with CF (Figure 1.1).

The thick mucus also plugs the tubes and passages in the pancreas, a gland that secretes enzymes that are essential for normal digestion. Poor digestion can cause abdominal pain and discomfort, as well as **diarrhea** and/or **constipation**. These conditions often cause serious malnutrition, resulting in delayed growth and development as well as chronic weight loss. Good nutrition and **replacement-enzyme** therapy are vital parts of a CF patient's long-term care.

WHAT ARE GENES AND CHROMOSOMES?

The mutated CFTR gene is passed from parent to child. Genes are the basic units of heredity that carry all of the detailed information that creates a human being and is passed on from parent to child. An estimated 20,000 to 25,000 genes live in the human body and transmit every characteristic from generation to generation. The word *gene* actually refers to a segment of **deoxyribonucleic acid (DNA)**, a **molecule** that stores genetic information. At life's most basic level, genes carry the instructions for making a single **protein** (or part of a protein) that create an individual's unique characteristics.

DNA is wrapped into strands called **chromosomes** and then wound tightly around certain proteins that will maintain the chromosome's form (Figure 1.2). These minute blueprints for life reside in a cell's control center, called the **nucleus**. (Cells are the basic units in all forms of life, including humans.) Genes carry different codes for different traits, such as skin and eye color. Occasionally, a change in a gene, called a mutation, occurs. Not all mutations are harmful, and some mutations are actually beneficial, but the mutated CFTR gene is especially dangerous because it can cause cystic fibrosis or be passed on to future offspring and increase their risk of having CF.

For a child to be born with CF, he or she must inherit two mutated CFTR genes—one from each parent. That implies that each parent is carrying a mutated gene and each has passed a copy of their mutated gene on to the child. If only one parent carries a mutated CFTR gene along with a normal one, and the other parent carries only two normal genes, the child will not have the disease. In that case, the child becomes a CF **carrier**. (The genetics of CF will be discussed in Chapter 3.)

DNA, Genes, and Chromosomes

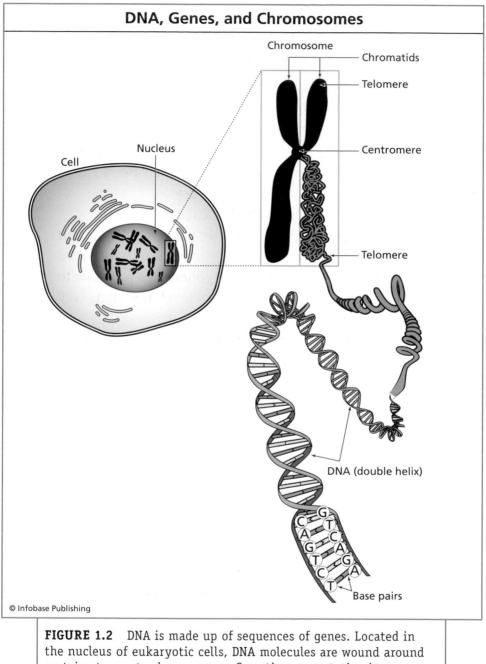

Chromosome

Chromatids

Telomere

Centromere

Telomere

Nucleus

Cell

DNA (double helix)

Base pairs

© Infobase Publishing

FIGURE 1.2   DNA is made up of sequences of genes. Located in the nucleus of eukaryotic cells, DNA molecules are wound around proteins to create chromosomes. Sometimes a mutation in a gene may cause diseases and/or disorders, such as cystic fibrosis.

LIVING WITH CYSTIC FIBROSIS

To the person living with cystic fibrosis, working to stay healthy becomes a highly important effort. Most CF patients must:

- Carefully monitor what they eat to maintain a high-fat, high-calorie diet. With today's conventional wisdom that people need less dietary **fat**, why does a CF patient need a high-fat diet? Because fat has twice the calories (9 per gram) of proteins (4 per gram) and **carbohydrates** (4 per gram). Thus, fat produces twice the energy per weight unit (grams) of either proteins or carbohydrates. And a CF patient needs as much energy as possible to support optimal growth and development as well as lung health. Carbohydrates and proteins also provide energy, and each plays additional roles in body function. Carbohydrates, which are found in starch, sugar, and fiber (e.g., breads and cereals), eventually change into blood glucose (a type of sugar) that all cells need for their growth and functions. Proteins play vital roles in the body, as well. They provide structure for red blood cells, help the body's natural antibodies to resist infection, and support growth and repair of body tissues, among other functions.
- Take pancreatic **replacement enzymes** with meals and snacks. Because the pancreas cannot function normally to aid digestion, CF patients must take replacement enzymes that work in the intestinal tract to digest food and support nutrient absorption.
- Take extra vitamins and minerals as needed. Vitamins A, D, E, and K are **fat-soluble vitamins** that

are not absorbed well in CF patients because of a damaged pancreas. Vitamins are essential for regulating body processes, including growth and bone structure.

◆ Avoid exposure to germs. Any infection can put lungs and airways at risk for losing more of their existing function. Germs are everywhere throughout the environment, so CF patients need to learn how to avoid damage from exposure to germs. Patients must thoroughly wash their hands after touching anything in a public environment (such as magazines, books, toilet, and door handles, for example). Hand washing removes many germs that patients may inadvertently pick up. Patients also need to avoid contact with anyone who is ill with a cough, cold, influenza, or any other contagious disease.

◆ Get a flu shot. A flu shot can impart immunity to the most common strains of influenza virus expected to flourish during a specific flu season. Each year, the World Health Organization (WHO) gathers and analyzes the previous year's viral influenza strains. WHO gathers information from 122 influenza centers in 94 countries (including the United States) and then projects which strains are most likely to circulate globally in the coming flu season. The chosen viral strains are then used to make that year's flu shot.

◆ Not smoke, and avoid exposure to secondhand smoke from others who do smoke.

◆ Clear the airways by correctly using prescribed drugs that are given by aerosol; that is, inhaled as a mist via a nebulizer. A nebulizer is a machine that has a small cup attached to a small air compressor that shoots air through the cup to change the medication into a mist. Patients inhale the mist from a mask or mouthpiece. Medication for lungs can also be given a single dose at a time (called a metered dose) through a metered-dose inhaler. Here, the patient breathes in while squeezing a small unit that fits in the mouth and contains the medication.

◆ Maintain as high a level of physical activity as possible. Exercise increases air exchange in and out of the lungs, which in turn supports keeping airways open and lungs functioning at the best levels possible in an individual patient.

Colin's Life with CF

Colin Maydahl is 25 years old, and as far back as he can remember, has been aware that he has CF. His mother told him early on about the disease and its symptoms. When he was young, the diagnosis meant little to him. The grave nature of the disease did not hit home until a sixth-grade classmate came to Colin one day crying, telling Colin that he would die soon. "Her parents had told her that I would die soon. I had an idea about what the norm for CF was, but it didn't hit home until then," Colin said. "I knew that my lungs would kill me someday, but her parents had old information. That happens a lot with people who know little about CF."

To Colin, keeping an optimistic attitude and being physically active are highly important and help him feel normal and strong. During his childhood, he stayed very active and played baseball and ran races. Socializing with friends added richness and fun to his life, even though by late elementary school he frequently missed school because of doctors' appointments.

(continues on page 18)

FROM ANCIENT MALADY TO GENETIC KNOWLEDGE

During the 1600s, reports emerged of newborns showing characteristic signs and symptoms of what is now known as cystic fibrosis. At the time, people did not understand that these abnormalities were part of a specific disease, but they knew that babies showing these signs and symptoms would soon die. A baby's salty skin was one strong indicator to these people that the infant was seriously ill: An individual who licked the baby's skin got a strong salty taste. (Today, we know that a baby with CF carries an internal overload of salt, some of which is secreted through the skin as perspiration.) Digestive problems commonly emerged, as well. Babies with this disorder passed greasy, massive **stools** from their **bowels** and had painful, distended bellies. These conditions led to a failure to thrive and the infant's early death.

In that era, people were frightened and bewildered when infants showed these signs and symptoms. The community considered these newborns "bewitched" or "hexed" because they usually died within days or months after showing signs and symptoms of the diseases. Even centuries before the 1600s, folklore and old songs suggested that CF symptoms were quite common in Caucasian babies. "Babies with salty foreheads will soon die" became a common belief. Only centuries later would the condition become a recognized disease.

That recognition came in the 1930s. First, scientist Guido Fanconi described the symptoms as a gastrointestinal syndrome. Then, in 1938, Columbia University pathologist and researcher Dorothy Andersen developed the first comprehensive report that described the malady as a discrete disease, which she named cystic fibrosis. Her pioneering research journey began when, as she conducted an autopsy on a deceased child, she noticed a lesion on a child's pancreas. This young person had been diagnosed with celiac disease, a then-recognized illness caused by intestinal hypersensitivity to gluten, a condition that inhibits digestion. Intrigued, she began to conduct an extensive search of autopsy records and whatever medical literature she could find that might offer insights and information about this pancreatic lesion and its relationship to celiac disease. A clear pattern emerged from her analysis, a pattern of clinical illness that until then had not been recognized. Her landmark report, "Cystic Fibrosis of the Pancreas and Its Relation to Celiac Disease: A Clinical and Pathologic Study," became a landmark study on which future CF researchers would build.

The understanding of CF advanced significantly when, in 1989, the CF gene was discovered. That milestone resulted from the growth of knowledge since the discovery of genes in the 1800s. An Austrian monk, Gregor Mendel, began to study varieties of pea plants during the early part of that century. As his work developed, he recognized that "paired hereditary units," as he called them, carried the individual characteristics of various lines of pea plants and maintained consistency within each pea variety. His 1866 paper detailing the results of his work proved a pivotal event in scientific understanding of heredity, and the world of science has credited Mendel with the discovery of genes.

Since then, genetic knowledge has grown enormously, as researchers around the world continue to conduct studies into the deepest corners of genetic function (see Chapter 3). That knowledge resulted in identification of the cystic fibrosis gene.

(continues)

(continued)

Medical understanding of the multiple aspects of CF has grown, too. Much of that knowledge has given rise to improving a CF patient's life. For example, in the 1950s, as CF and its symptoms became better understood, the need for medical, psychological, and sociological support for patients emerged. Specialized CF clinics were developed around the United States to serve as a centralized resource for diagnosis and treatment of CF patients and social support for their families. Many of those clinics remain operational today.

Although CF research continued during the 1960s, children with the disease continued to die young, and most died by adolescence. They suffered miserably during their short lifetimes. But living with CF became easier in the 1970s as new therapies and treatments were developed, including the introduction of breathing devices and dietary changes. Medical professionals were often skeptical about the effectiveness of these new treatments. However, when they saw that these new therapies actually improved a patient's quality of life and significantly increased their longevity, using these novel treatments

(continued from page 15)

His mother constantly worried about his condition, he said. Sometimes, however, his disease made his school-age years easier for him. Colin would manipulate his situation to avoid school. "It was not very hard to get a stay-at-home-from-school pass," he said. "But that came back to bite me . . . because now I cannot spell to save my life." During his childhood, Colin had no serious problems, although he continued to be closely monitored by his doctor.

to control disease symptoms became professionally accepted as good medical practice.

The 1980s were exciting years for CF researchers as they developed a deeper understanding of human genetics. The race was on to find the exact gene that caused CF. But identifying the gene proved a difficult journey. Finally, in 1989, two researchers isolated the damaged gene. Scientists knew this gene affected normal **chloride channel function**. Chloride channels help move salt and water back and forth across cell walls. Therefore, the gene was named the cystic fibrosis transmembrane conductance regulator gene, or CFTR. The possibility of curing CF, as well as many other genetic diseases, via **gene therapy** has grown into a research area of intense focus. To date, researchers have discovered more than 15,000 mutations in the CF gene, and they continue to work on finding ways to fix the damaged gene. If fixing the CFTR gene becomes possible, prevention and cure of CF may become a reality.

One constant thread for recognizing this disease has weaved its way from early centuries to today. As sophisticated as treatments and therapies have become, having salty skin still remains diagnostic for CF.

Today, CF patients such as Colin have access to good doctors and increasingly effective therapies. The knowledge about cystic fibrosis has grown enormously over the past century as new tools and technologies emerged—especially in **genetics**. Treatment methods to successfully maintain optimal lung function and control CF symptoms as much as possible have become increasingly sophisticated. Support groups for patients and families are widely available. Ongoing research into the cause and possible cure of this fatal disease offer CF patients the ways and means for feeling better, as well as hope for a possible cure and/or prevention of the disease.

All of the above advances are relatively recent. For centuries, people knew that something was wrong with babies that had salty skin and died early, but only in the last century was cystic fibrosis recognized as a defined disease entity.

Learning to Cope

When Colin was 13 years old, he came down with the flu and permanently lost some of his lung function. Never again would he breathe as easily as he once did. Still, he took up mountain biking "to keep me off the couch and in an active lifestyle. It helped me keep my head up, rather than feeling down. It helped me feel normal, even if I was coughing my lungs out," he said.

Racing mountain bikes, bungee jumping, skydiving, surfing, rock climbing, and traveling kept Colin busy and in good spirits whenever he was physically able to participate. Little by little, however, he became increasingly short of breath. "I have always given it my all not to let CF hold me back from doing anything," he said. "But surfing is too aerobic now, and my lungs cannot keep up. I still rock climb and travel. It is only now that I'm 25 that my lungs are slowing down from doing anything [highly] physical. I will still give [an activity] a go, and most of the time I can do it, even though I might be just a little slower."

Colin received a trip to Australia from his father as a high school graduation gift. But he had to cut the journey short when he began to lose weight. He has since traveled the world extensively, as his health permits, despite the challenges of finding food he can eat, avoiding contact with other people, and resting as needed. He watches his CF symptoms carefully, and his health concerns are always with him. Inexpensive travel, such as staying in youth hostels, is challenging because he coughs so much at night and because hostels bring him in contact with too many people, a common source of disease exposure. To people with CF, like Colin, any exposure to germs and viruses is worrisome because they can contract lung infections so easily. While traveling in Thailand, he got sick from digestive problems and slept about 14 hours a day; it also took a long time for him to recover from that event.

Symptoms in cystic fibrosis patients usually worsen with age, and Colin is no exception. But as physical activity became increasingly difficult, a new door opened that added to his zest for life. Ever since he was a teenager, Colin had yearned to own and ride a motorcycle, though his father had rejected the idea because of his concerns for Colin's safety. Colin's dream, however, finally became a reality after a family friend changed his father's mind by pointing out that Colin had been through so much misery that he deserved to realize his dream. Colin's father reversed his opinion and bought a motorcycle for him, and now Colin rides his motorcycle every chance he can. "I love it. It makes me forget about my lungs. I'm so hooked," he said.

Is a Love Life Possible?

Many young people seek out a special person to go on dates with and have fun. Colin is no different. Girlfriends have come and gone in his life, however. He has always been open with people about his condition, he explains, but sometimes that honesty backfires. Often, people with CF cannot have children, and Colin says that he has "dated a few girls who didn't like that I could not have kids, or thought I was 'damaged.' They are ex-girlfriends for a reason. With relationships, I worry that I won't be loved because I don't have a normal life expectancy. I can't have kids in the normal fashion, which is something I'm okay with because I would want to be able to support my family and be there for my kids as they grew up. And I'm not sure that can happen. I worry about dying alone." His current girlfriend is a good companion, he said, and "loves me for being me."

Facts of the Matter

While Colin's reference to a shortened life expectancy is correct, advances in treatments have added many years to CF patients' life spans. In 1938, when cystic fibrosis was first described as a specific disease, the life expectancy was six months. Only a few decades ago, many CF patients failed to reach age 20. But with medical and scientific advances— including synthetic drugs such as Pulmozyme that thins the mucus and makes it easier for patients to cough the mucus up—today's life expectancy for an individual with CF is about age 35, and many now live past age 40. Many new therapies are in testing stages and will be discussed later in detail.

Colin's statement that he cannot have kids is based on fact. Most men with CF suffer from **infertility** because they lack the duct called the **vas deferens** that transports sperm from inside to outside of the body. Today, however, new fertility methods and surgical procedures can often restore male fertility. Women with CF have fewer problems with infertility. They may be a little less fertile than other women, but their internal reproductive organs (ovaries and uterus) are intact, and so they can usually conceive and experience successful pregnancies. However, women with CF face the possibility that their CF symptoms will worsen during pregnancy. They need optimal care while pregnant and frequent observations by their health-care providers.

Choosing a Path

Young people like Colin face important decisions as they grow into adulthood. Finding a good job and/or going to

FRÉDÉRIC CHOPIN: A SUFFERING GENIUS

Frédéric Chopin, the brilliant Polish composer and pianist of the 1800s, suffered multiple maladies throughout his short life. His doctors diagnosed him as having tuberculosis, and that diagnosis lasted for nearly two centuries after he died. Only in the past few decades have scholars begun to question this long-accepted assumption.

Many experts now believe that Frédéric Chopin, the famous composer and pianist, had cystic fibrosis.

Today, many experts hypothesize that Chopin actually suffered from cystic fibrosis. For one, he endured serious, chronic respiratory disease from childhood onward. Repeated and increasingly severe lung infections plagued him as years passed. In letters and notes of the 1800s, Chopin was described as a delicate, emaciated person with sunken cheeks who weighed less than 100 pounds (45 kilograms, or kg) throughout adulthood. He suffered from chronic bouts of abdominal pain and diarrhea, especially after eating fatty foods like pork. He consistently lost weight after eating any foods that disagreed with his digestive tract and after episodes of acute lung infections. His growth and development were severely impaired, and he complained at age 22 that he had little to no facial hair. While he had several relationships with women, no children resulted, suggesting that he may have been infertile.

(continues)

(continued)

Despite his unceasing and overwhelming misery, the maestro continued to compose, perform, and teach. He finally became so weak that he could not climb stairs and needed to be carried off the stage after a performance. Although he continued to teach piano, during the final four years of his life he had to teach lying down. Chopin's friends provided the physical care he needed during that time. In the last year of his life, Chopin remained bedridden, which gave rise to a host of additional physical problems. His legs and ankles swelled, he fought mightily to cough up the thick mucus buried deep in his lungs, and he became increasingly exhausted. He died in agony at age 39.

college are two big issues. People with CF often have challenges in the workplace, including bosses' and coworkers' tolerance for the repeated lung infections that cause routine hospitalizations. Energy and stress levels are other challenges on the job. Can the employee with CF, who often tires easily, cope with change, manage disagreeable colleagues, and adjust to high-stress situations? In addition, because a CF patient's energy level diminishes over time, he or she may no longer be physically able do certain job tasks. They may need special physical help and adjustments to their work environments, too.

Colin has experienced some of these obstacles. For a short time, he studied at a junior college, but he became ill halfway through the first semester and missed several weeks of school. That gap put him significantly behind in his classes. He decided that higher education probably would not suit his needs anyway, because he likely could not hold down a full-time job after finishing school. "Why would an employer keep me on if I had to take a few weeks off five or six times a year?" he questions.

Might the Americans With Disabilities Act (ADA) of 1990 protect any job that Colin may take on, despite his necessary extended time off the job? Although the act prohibits employers from discriminating against any citizen "with a physical or mental impairment that substantially limits one or more major life activities," according to the U.S. Equal Employment Opportunity Commission, this protection is not an employer's responsibility if the disabled person's needs impose an "undue hardship" on the functioning of an employer's business. Therefore, the ADA may not cover Colin's frequent, extended absences from a job.

Yet Colin does have a job. Since age 16, he has worked part-time at a bicycle shop. He loves the work, and the position is flexible. His work waits for him after he returns from his bouts in the hospital. "Stopping my life so I can spend a few weeks in the hospital is harder than just doing the hospital time," he said. "It's stopping and restarting a routine that is difficult."

Attitude and Experience

At 25 years old, Colin spends more time now in hospitals than he has in the past. Over the past three years, he has been hospitalized five to seven times a year for up to three weeks at a time. He is often admitted for lung infections, and sometimes for extreme fatigue, as well as for showing low levels of lung function.

"People think I have a great outlook on life, and I guess I do," Colin said. "But people never know what they can do until it is put in front of them. One of my best friends recently named his son after me, and I have never felt so touched."

SIGNS, SYMPTOMS, AND DIAGNOSIS

Cystic fibrosis claims more lives than any other genetic disease, according to Stanford University's Cystic Fibrosis Center. To date, a cure does not exist. Because of the thick, gluey mucus in the lungs of a person with cystic fibrosis, breathing in and out is very difficult. The sticky mucus not only blocks air passageways, it also plugs up the ducts of the pancreas, a large gland that lies behind the stomach and secretes hormones and digestive enzymes (Figure 2.1).

These enzymes are necessary for digesting carbohydrates, proteins, and fats. They also ensure that important vitamins are absorbed. Without the enzymes, many individuals with CF have serious digestive problems and suffer from malnutrition. Some people with CF, however, have only a partial mutation in the CFTR gene that causes CF and may retain some normal internal functions. Therefore, signs and symptoms of CF differ according to the severity of an individual's disease. For example, one person may have lung problems but not digestive problems, and vice versa. Also, aging can affect CF signs and symptoms. Tests can be given throughout the life of a person with CF to help track the changes in an individual's condition.

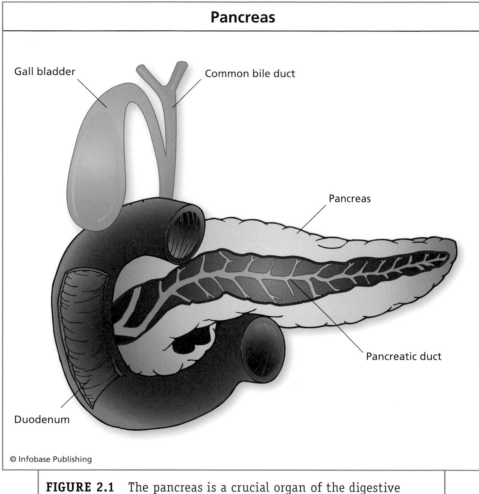

Pancreas

Gall bladder

Common bile duct

Pancreas

Pancreatic duct

Duodenum

© Infobase Publishing

FIGURE 2.1   The pancreas is a crucial organ of the digestive system. The thick, sticky mucus caused by the mutated CFTR gene plugs up the ducts of the pancreas.

NEWBORNS

Newborns with CF may not show symptoms immediately. If they do, one common symptom is blocked intestines, which prevents the normal passage of **meconium**, a sticky, greenish material that is the first stool that healthy infants pass in the first few days after birth. Also, babies with CF may fail to grow, suffer frequent respiratory infections, and pass bulky, greasy stools. If any of these signs appear, the physician may take a blood sample and do a genetic analysis to confirm the diagnosis.

CHILDREN AND YOUNG ADULTS

A person kissing a child's forehead or arm can quickly pick up a common sign of CF—salty skin. As discussed in Chapter 1, having salty skin was the first sign of what people centuries ago knew only as a strange malady. The skin is salty because CF patients have higher than normal amounts of sodium chloride, or salt, in their sweat.

Children and young adults can also show the same bowel symptoms as infants prior to diagnosis. Slowed growth patterns, wheezing, and the coughing up of thick **sputum** from the lungs may also show up. Reoccurring **pneumonia** often results from continual lung and **sinus** infections. Enlarged, rounded fingertips and toes—a condition called clubbing—eventually occurs in almost all people with CF. Why this is so is not well understood, though many researchers point to the poor lung function of CF patients, which results in abnormal oxygenation throughout the body. That results in poor circulation of oxygen, especially to distant body parts such as fingers and toes.

Nasal polyps are also common in children and older people with CF. Polyps are stalk-like growths that protrude from membrane linings, such as the nose or intestines. No one knows why the polyps occur, although studies show that they are associated quite strongly with cystic fibrosis. Even if they are surgically removed, the polyps tend to recur. Besides the thick mucus that blocks airways, nasal polyps

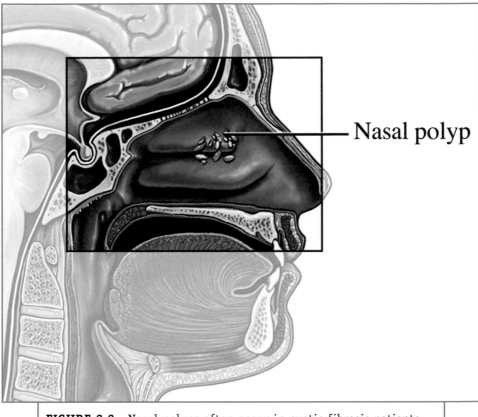

Nasal polyp

FIGURE 2.2   Nasal polyps often occur in cystic fibrosis patients and interfere with breathing.

may also interfere with a CF patient's ability to breathe normally (Figure 2.2).

Cirrhosis of the liver can also occur in people with CF. This frequently fatal condition is caused by liver inflammation and/or clogged bile ducts. The liver is the largest gland in the human body and weighs from 2.5 pounds to 5 pounds (1.13 to 2.27 kg) in an adult. This gland performs many critical functions, including secreting **bile**, a yellow green fluid that helps digest, or break down, and absorb fat. The liver also filters harmful microorganisms and toxins from the blood. If the normal free flow of fluids and bile becomes impeded, the liver hardens to the point that it can no longer function properly. That lack of function can cause a patient to die.

POLYPS: AN AGE-OLD PROBLEM

As far back as 1000 B.C., people in India were removing nasal polyps with scoops or rings. In 400 B.C., the Greek physician **Hippocrates** described these polyps and developed several ways to remove them. First, he developed a sponge technique: He used a rough sponge, tied it to a string, inserted it completely through the nose, and then jerked the growths out of the nose. In his writings, he also described using hot irons to sear and destroy the polyps' tissue. Hippocrates also conceived the idea of removing polyps with a snare. Here, he looped the snare around the polyps, and then pulled them out.

Snare removal is still used today, though other surgical methods of removal are more common. Physicians will sometimes use forceps (clamps) to pull out polyps. Another technique is to use a long tube called an **endoscope** that is inserted into the nose to locate and remove the growths. However, today's treatment for polyps usually begins by applying **steroid medications** directly to the growths or by taking oral steroid medications. Steroid medications are powerful anti-inflammatory substances that can prevent inflammation of nasal linings, which contributes to formation of nasal polyps. Currently, surgical removal is often the last resort in treating nasal polyps. Today, people with CF frequently require repeated surgical removal of these polyps because they frequently grow back and interfere with the ability to breathe through the nose.

DIAGNOSIS

Some diagnostic tests for CF, such as the sweat test, have been around for years. Other tests that rely on genetic analysis have become available only recently. In 2005, the U.S. Food and Drug Administration (FDA) approved the first DNA-based test for cystic fibrosis. Today's diagnostic testing for CF primarily consists of one or more of the following procedures. A diagnostician selects which test or tests are most appropriate for an individual.

Sweat Chloride Test

For years, the sweat chloride test, which measures the amount of sodium chloride in a person's sweat, has been the standard test for CF. In this test, a small amount of a sweat-producing chemical is put on an area of a person's arm or leg. An **electrode** is then attached, which creates a weak electrical current. After a few minutes, the process stimulates sweat production. The sample goes to a laboratory, where the levels of salt, or sodium chloride, in the sweat are measured. If abnormally high levels of sodium choride are present, the person may have CF. At that point, additional diagnostic tests are typically conducted to confirm the diagnosis.

Immunoreactive Trypsinogen

This analysis is used for newborns because they often produce too little sweat to be measured by the sweat test. Two to three days after birth, blood samples are taken and analyzed for increased levels of a pancreatic enzyme called immunoreactive **trypsinogen** (IRT). Findings of increased IRT levels, however, may or may not be a strong indicator of CF. Other neonatal conditions that impair pancreatic function also show high levels of the enzyme. Infants with intestinal malformations and/or conditions such as bowel obstruction are two such examples. Therefore, to confirm a diagnosis of CF, additional testing must be done. Gene mutation analysis is often the test of choice because it can reveal mutations in the CFTR gene, which is clear evidence that an individual has CF.

DNA Mutation Analysis

DNA mutation analysis comprises a variety of genetic testing methods that, in the case of cystic fibrosis, look for the presence of the many mutations in the CFTR gene. These tests are increasingly used to help confirm the CF diagnosis because their results are becoming highly specific. How is a DNA analysis performed? First, the DNA is isolated and purified from cells taken from a blood sample or from a smear inside the cheek. Called a buccal smear, this noninvasive cell-sample gathering is performed by using a small spatula to scrape the inside of the cheek. From there, a variety of methods are used to detect disease genes and identify mutations within a specific DNA sequence. These methods are discussed below.

DNA Microarray

DNA microarray technology is a new method of mutation analysis, developed only in the past few years. Among its many uses, the microarray method is proving highly useful for pinpointing the mutations in the CFTR gene. In a DNA microarray study, thousands of molecules or molecular fragments of DNA, called genetic probes or chips, are arranged in a predetermined way to adhere to a glass slide or silicon chip. This kind of study allows scientists to identify which particular genes are active, which genes are active at a low level, and which genes are inactive. This knowledge aids researchers in understanding how cells function normally and how these cells are affected when certain genes fail to function normally.

Because the slide holds an enormous number of DNA pieces, scientists can study the expression of a full set of genes that make up a particular genome. The first step in conducting a DNA microarray study is to find out which genes are turned on and which are turned off in a selected cell. To do so, the researcher must first gather the cell's messenger RNA (mRNA) molecules. (A cell's mRNA provides a cell's map for creating proteins.) The scientist does this by tweaking a cell's normal function. Once a gene from the cell is activated, the cell goes into action and starts to copy specific segments of that gene. The end product of this cellular process is the mRNA. The scientist then culls the mRNA, tags it with **fluorescent dye**, and places the tagged mRNA onto a DNA microarray slide. Once on the slide, the mRNA from the cell will bind to its complementary DNA already on the microarray and leave its calling card, the fluorescent color it was tagged with.

The scientist then uses a specialized scanner to measure the fluorescent places on the microarray and how bright they are. Places that are highly brilliant indicate that this particular gene is active. A dimmer shine indicates that a gene is somewhat active. If an area shows no color at all, that gene is inactive. Knowing these varying levels of gene activity can help scientists pursue new knowledge about a disease. In cystic fibrosis, DNA microarray studies can help find out how drugs work in cells, and what gene products may be therapeutic or perhaps good targets themselves for further therapeutic research.

DNA microarray shows promise in both infant screening and genetic testing for CF. It can measure **gene expression** levels within a single genome. Gene expression is the

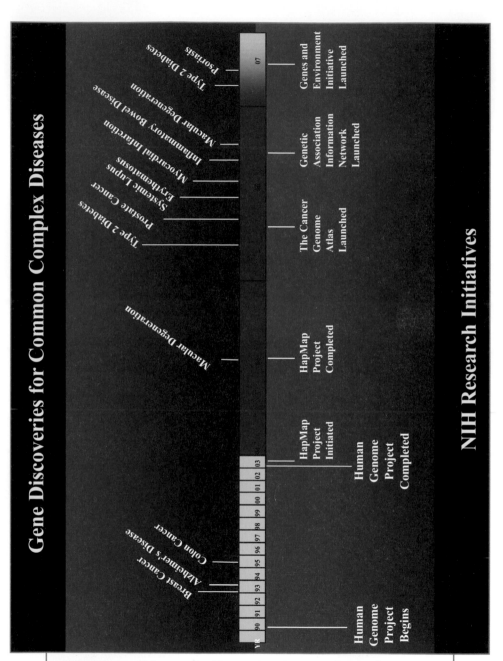

FIGURE 2.3 This genetic discoveries timeline shows when each disease-causing gene was identified, from the beginning of the Human Genome Project in 1990 to 2007.

process that uses the encoded instructions in DNA to make proteins. This technology can detect all of the thousands of mutations within a CFTR gene in one test. Fast detection of CFTR mutations has sparked medical interest in eventually using a single DNA microarray to accurately screen infants for CF. A single test also allows genetic testing to be done quickly.

Today's researchers aim to identify CF-related genes in order to develop disease biomarkers. Biomarkers are detectable cellular or **metabolic** indicators of change within a biological system. Biomarkers are useful because they can be measured. By identifying CF-related genes, researchers may have the ability to use measured changes as biomarkers in CF lung gene therapy. CF biomarkers may show that an episode of gene therapy has worked for a patient. How? DNA microarray technology emerged from the sequencing of the human genome via the **Human Genome Project (HGP)**, which was completed in 2003 (Figure 2.3). Older methods of genetic study restricted scientists to "seeing" one or two genes of interest in a life form, including humans. Today, DNA microarrays gather highly specific information in genetic and in other biochemical analyses. Its uses will likely expand as it produces increasingly successful studies.

Lung X-rays and Function Tests

Lung function tests measure the amount of air the lungs can hold, how fast a person can exhale, and how well the lungs add oxygen to and remove carbon dioxide from the blood. A chest X-ray can show lung scarring from recurrent inflammations. Although these tests do not confirm a diagnosis of CF, they help in evaluating the severity of an individual's lung damage. By repeating these tests over time, the physician can track changes in the lungs.

Sinus X-rays

The pictures can reveal signs of **sinusitis**, which indicates an infection and/or inflammation of these nasal cavities. When sinus X-rays show sinusitis, finding the underlying cause becomes important. Many conditions can trigger sinusitis, including allergies or a patient's poorly functioning immune system. Sweat chloride tests are often conducted. Positive test results can be added to other accumulating evidence and eventually support a diagnosis of CF or rule it out.

Sputum Cultures

By examining a sample of a person's **phlegm**, the physician can learn what kinds of microorganisms are thriving there. ***Aspergillus fumigatus***, for example, is a common fungus that often appears in sputum cultures from people with CF. Finding the fungus in a person's test can add specific information to the body of evidence as the doctor seeks a diagnosis of CF or another ailment. ***Pseudomonas aeruginosa*** is the most common bacteria in the lungs of a person with CF. Therefore, discovering these bacteria in an undiagnosed person's sputum can add important information to the mass of prediagnosis information. For years, sputum tests have been a part of the diagnostic process, but their use is lessening since the advent of recent high-tech developments such as gene testing. However, sputum tests remain an important part of routine checkups for people with CF because they can reveal specific infections in the lungs or the airways.

Nasal Passage Potential Differences

Individuals with CF can show an abnormal movement of salt across cell walls in the nasal passages. The nasal passage test uses electrodes to measure the rate at which salt flows in and out of nasal cells. People with CF often show different **voltage measurements** than people without CF. (Voltage is a kind of pressure that forces electrical charges through a circuit.) Measuring that possible difference in a person's nasal passages may give the doctor significant information that can help confirm a CF diagnosis.

Genotyping

Genotyping, or gene testing, is a process used to determine all or part of the genetic makeup of an individual or group. Gene testing is useful in diagnosing CF and in narrowing down a patient's specific CF mutations, which helps to determine the level of risk for organ dysfunction. For example, the Johns Hopkins University DNA Diagnostic Laboratory can conduct a variety of tests for individual patients and/or their families. They include:

◆ CFTR sequencing tests for identifying mutations in the CFTR gene.

◆ **Prenatal** diagnosis that shows whether or not the fetus has CF or is a carrier. This laboratory test is more sensitive than most routine American CF lab panels (e.g., the numbers of specific tests run on one blood or smear sample from a patient). The heightened sensitivity can pick up rare CF mutations that most routine CF lab panels cannot.

◆ Targeted mutation testing, which is useful for carrier testing in families with known CFTR mutations. The test also serves to confirm a mutation identified in a research setting or from a clinical lab outside of the United States.

◆ The newest test at Johns Hopkins DNA laboratory analyzes a specific CF mutation (called 5-thymidine, or 5T) that varies in how much it affects the mutated CFTR gene. Testing involves analyzing 5T along with another CF mutation. Test results show that these two combined mutations can cause a variety of **phenotypes**. These include male infertility (resulting from the absence of the vas deferens), normal CFTR phenotypes, and rare types of CF. These results can show the influence of CF disease risk.

COMPLICATIONS OF CYSTIC FIBROSIS

Individual CF patients face differing challenges, depending on the severity of their disease. Besides their day-to-day care, such as keeping breathing tubes open by loosening lung mucus, patients sometimes experience complications of their disease.

THE RISK OF DIABETES

Several factors increase the risk of **diabetes** in an individual with CF. Factors include pancreas damage, a lessened sensitivity to **insulin**, and/or genetic reasons. Over time, a specialized part of the pancreas, the insulin-making islet cells, may cease to function normally. As a result, islet cells lose their ability to control blood sugar levels, and a patient may become partially or fully insulin resistant. When that happens, a person with CF may first become **glucose intolerant**, a condition often called prediabetes. Here glucose (sugar) levels may fluctuate, leading to either hypoglycemic (too little) or hyperglycemic (too much) levels of blood sugar. This leads to the inability to use or store food in the body's cells and a rise or decline in blood sugar. High levels of blood sugar can lead to serious damage to many parts of the body.

In CF patients, regular blood or urine measurement of glucose levels may show normal results; a fully diabetic state is difficult to pin down. The most reliable test is the **oral glucose tolerance**

Lung Infections

Lung infections are very common with CF and usually occur many times during a CF patient's lifetime. *Pseudomonas aeruginosa* is a bacterium that can cause a variety of problems, including pneumonia, chronic sinusitis, **bronchitis**, and bronchiectasis, in which the walls of the bronchial tubes become too wide or dilated. This condition makes it harder for a person with CF to clear their airways, which then become infected.

Pseudomonas aeruginosa is called an opportunistic pathogen. This means that the bacteria can invade and multiply quickly in any broken or injured area of the body. The

test. Here, the person drinks a sugar solution, then has his or her blood sugar level measured immediately and then measured again two hours later. Treatment for prediabetics often involves weight loss and dietary changes that help keep blood glucose levels within a tolerable range. Treatment for full-blown diabetes usually involves substantial diet adjustments, timing of meals, and administration of insulin and/or oral medications. Routine monitoring of blood sugar levels with a blood glucose meter is critical to make sure that glucose levels stay within a healthy range. Experts at Stanford University's Cystic Fibrosis Center recommend yearly blood glucose testing of all people with CF over age sixteen. An A1C test is also useful for routinely monitoring a patient's blood sugar level. This test accurately measures the average blood glucose level over the previous two to three months to give a broad view of a patient's state of blood sugar control over time. The A1C test is usually performed several times a year in a laboratory or by using a home testing kit.

CF patient's damaged breathing passages and injured lungs offer these bacteria easy access and a suitable environment for growth. The infection can quickly take over many body systems and cause serious harm. The presence of *Pseudomonas aeruginosa* is rare in healthy people, largely because a healthy individual's intact skin and body organs offer these organisms no entry point. Yet sometimes these bacteria will grow into colonies in moist body sites of normally healthy people who become ill, especially those with pneumonia or other structural lung problems (such as bronchiectasis) that weaken their immune systems. Other body sites that may attract these bacteria include the gastrointestinal tract, throat, nasal mucosa, and perineum. It is important to note that people harboring *Pseudomonas aeruginosa* are not contagious to others.

Asthma

This is a chronic respiratory disease in which the bronchial airways of the lungs become narrowed, making it difficult to breathe. Asthma can appear in patients with CF when the bronchial linings become chronically inflamed. A lung may collapse from the effects of wear and tear, chronic irritation due to infection, and long-term breathing difficulties resulting from CF. When collapse occurs, air leaks out of the lungs and into the chest cavity. Over time, lung disease may cause heart failure. Eventually, worsening lung problems can result in death for many people with CF.

Nutritional Problems

Serious nutritional deficiencies and chronic diarrhea are two common problems in people with CF. Malnutrition is caused by the mucus secretions that obstruct the pancreatic ducts. Because the ducts are blocked, the pancreatic enzymes that normally digest fats and proteins can no longer reach the intestines. That means that people with CF also cannot absorb the fat-soluble vitamins A, D, E, and K. Also, if the liver's bile duct is plugged, inflammation may develop, which can lead to cirrhosis of the liver.

Reproductive Problems

Many men with CF are infertile because their bodies either cannot correctly form the vas deferens, the tube that **semen** passes through, or the tube becomes blocked. Therefore, a nonexistent or abnormal vas deferens prevents semen from reaching its destination to fertilize a woman's egg. However, with today's highly developed fertility treatments and surgical interventions, many men with CF are able to become fathers.

Most women with CF can become pregnant despite the effects of their disease. Most infertility problems occur because they have thicker cervical mucus than normal women. That makes it harder for sperm to push through to fertilize the woman's egg (**ovum**). Sometimes women with CF have small ovaries and uteruses compared to healthy women. Irregular menstrual cycles and decreased ovulation rates may also contribute to infertility. However, with today's medical advances (such as in vitro insemination) they usually can conceive and complete a full-term pregnancy. However, CF symptoms can worsen during pregnancy, so women with CF are encouraged to explore the risks with their doctors before deciding to get pregnant. Once they become pregnant, they need careful medical monitoring. Diabetes may appear, for example. They also may have trouble gaining enough weight during their gestation period.

GENETIC BASIS OF CYSTIC FIBROSIS

A gene is the basic physical unit of heredity that specifies characteristics in an individual. Some of the most obvious characteristics are eye color, hair color, and height. Genes do this by specifying the structure of a particular protein or proteins.

As a fundamental unit, genes form a sequence of molecules, called **nucleotides**, along a segment of deoxyribonucleic acid (DNA). These nucleotides provide coded instructions for making a substance called **RNA**, or **ribonucleic acid**. RNA translates into the production of proteins that determine an individual's characteristics. The human body's entire process of protein production derives from an individual's precise **genetic code**. The body's proteins help to determine the common traits that humans share, such as basic skeletal structure and body organs, as well as the individual traits that make people differ from each other, including facial characteristics and a person's fingerprints.

The human body contains an estimated 20,000 to 25,000 genes, and each cell carries two copies of almost all genes— one passed down from each parent. Each single gene is a distinct sequence of nucleotides that specifies one protein. Proteins are large organic compounds found in all living things. Proteins make up tissues and organs and are involved in many metabolic processes. They are also a necessary food substance for all animals, including humans. Built from subunits called **amino acids**, proteins help cells grow and divide, then stop them from growing too much. They also help repair body cells. Every cell and most body fluids contain proteins. Proteins carry out many specialized functions, such as building muscles, organs, and glands. Proteins are also necessary for maintaining the health of muscles, tendons, and **ligaments**. They also provide the means for human growth and development.

Proteins make up enzymes, which control all chemical reactions in the body. Enzymes are produced by living cells to allow cells to perform chemical reactions quickly. For example, enzymes control the metabolic process that converts food into energy and new cell material. Here are some examples:

◆ Pepsin, peptidases, and trypsin are enzymes that break down proteins into their respective amino acids.

◆ Lipases are enzymes that divide fats into glycerol and fatty acids.

◆ Amylases are enzymes that break down starch into simple sugars that the body can absorb and use for energy.

Enzymes also help transport materials across cell membranes.

GENES TURN OFF AND ON

In order for humans and other living organisms to grow and develop properly, a coordinated expression of genes at certain times and in specific places is required. In the 1950s and 1960s, researchers began to view genes as a group of plans—one plan for each protein. But further study revealed that genes do not manufacture their respective proteins all the time. So what turns genes on and off? In 1965, three researchers in France received the Nobel Prize for discovering a new class of genes called **operator genes**. These genes regulate cell metabolism by controlling production of certain enzymes. This pioneering work added significant new information to the world of genetics. It led to sweeping changes in the way scientists had perceived development of higher life forms, including humans. Now they can see that cells not only contain genetic plans inside their DNA for building structural proteins, but also house a genetic regulatory program that controls if and when these structural proteins will be built.

What Is a Genetic Mutation?

A gene mutation is a permanent change in a gene's DNA. A specific mutated gene, called the mutated CFTR gene, causes CF. Mutations occur in two basic ways: by the inheritance of a defective gene from one or both parents, or by the acquisition of an abnormal gene during the individual's lifetime.

Inherited Mutations

Inheriting genetic mutations from one or both parents indicates that the damaged gene permanently resides inside some of the woman's egg cells and/or some of a man's sperm cells. The damaged gene may then be passed down from parent to child. If so, the damaged gene remains in every cell of the child's body for a lifetime. CF is an example of a disease that is caused by inheriting two damaged CFTR genes—one from each parent.

Acquired Mutations

Cystic fibrosis is an inherited mutation, whereas acquired mutations are triggered by external forces, such as radiation or chemical exposures. Mutations can also be triggered by

EARLY DIAGNOSIS

Today's scientists have the tools to identify exact sequences of alleles on a specific gene—an important step in diagnosing CF. The damaged cystic fibrosis gene (the mutated CFTR gene) resides on chromosome 7. Its alleles present a distinctive pattern. Once revealed, that pattern confirms a diagnosis of CF. Advanced technologies allow a diagnosis of CF to be made while the fetus is still in the mother's womb. This capability is important to the health of an infant because treatment can begin as soon as the baby is born. That includes providing good nutrition to support weight gain, growth, and development. For example, CF patients often must take digestive enzymes that they lack to help them absorb nutrients effectively. If a newborn is known to have CF and has digestive problems, the supplemental digestive enzymes can be started right away to help the baby thrive.

Amniocentesis is one method used for early diagnosis. Here, a long, hollow needle is inserted through the wall of the mother's abdomen and into the uterus (Figure 3.1). A sample of amniotic fluid is withdrawn and tested for the presence of one or two CFTR mutations. A discovery of one CFTR mutation indicates that the fetus will be a CF carrier. If two CFTR mutations are found, a diagnosis of CF in the unborn child is confirmed.

Ultrasound imaging is another technology used today for many diagnostic examinations, including prenatal exams. Often parents-to-be request ultrasound imaging to find out the sex of the unborn child. In some cases, ultrasound can also be useful in showing the possibility that the fetus may have CF. Ultrasound uses high-frequency sound waves to make a moving visual image of the body area under study. The suspicion of fetal CF arises when the image shows a bright white area of the fetal

(continues)

(continued)

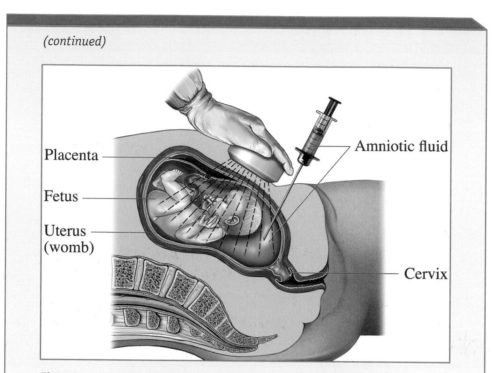

Placenta

Fetus

Uterus
(womb)

Amniotic fluid

Cervix

**Figure 3.1   In amniocentesis, a physician uses a needle to draw
a sample of amniotic fluid from the uterus. The physician uses
ultrasound in order to avoid contact with the fetus.**

bowel. That picture is called an echogenic fetal bowel image. Echogenic refers to a highly reactive response to ultrasound that appears as a bright white area and signals a possible malformation. Echogenic images can also reveal tumors of the heart and lungs, as well as growths in other organs.

foreign pathogens, such as viruses that bring on disease. A common acquired genetic mutation takes place in skin cells that are overexposed to the sun's radiation. This overexposure triggers mutations in skin cells that can lead to a variety of skin cancers.

Not all genetic mutations are harmful. Though most people have the same basic genes, a small number (less than 1%) of a human's total number of genes differs slightly between people. For many traits, there are different forms of the same gene, which are called **alleles**. The existence of two or more alleles for a trait is called a **polymorphism**. For example, multiple alleles determine blood type. One of the earliest identified polymorphisms consists of the **antigens** of the ABO blood group. Antigens are any matter foreign to the body that triggers an immune response. The antigens of the ABO blood group types of A, B, and AB, for example, pose potential harm to people receiving blood transfusions or undergoing **organ transplantation**. If the patient's blood type becomes mismatched with another blood type, the contact provokes such a strong reaction in blood vessel linings that the patient may suffer a severe, possibly deadly reaction. An ABO antigen mismatch during organ transplantation can also cause the body to reject the new organ. This rarely happens, because blood type is determined before a transfusion or an organ transplant.

WHAT ROLE DOES MUTATION PLAY IN CYSTIC FIBROSIS?

More than 900 mutations of the CFTR gene have been discovered. Normally, the CFTR gene works as a chloride channel, controlling the flow of sodium chloride (salt) and water in and out of body cells. A mutated CFTR gene, however, causes this flow to malfunction, disrupting the normal flow of salt and water between cells. This results in the **dehydration** of body secretions and production of the thick, sticky mucus that is characteristic of CF. Dehydration also causes the extreme loss of salt through body sweat—another primary symptom of CF.

For years, scientists have looked for the causes of CF. Finally, in 1989, researchers discovered that cystic fibrosis results from mutations of a specific gene, which we now know as the transmembrane conductance regulator gene, or CFTR gene. Dr. Francis S. Collins, a global expert in genetics and leader of the Human Genome Project, was a member of the research team that isolated the mutated CFTR gene.

HOW ARE GENES AND GENETIC DISEASES NAMED?

Naming genes is an important task. Imagine the confusion that would exist if two teams of researchers were studying the same gene but calling it by two different names. The **HUGO Gene Nomenclature Committee** is an international organization that aims to give a unique name and abbreviation to every human gene. So far, it has approved names for more than 13,000 genes of the estimated 30,000 genes in the human genome.

Unlike naming genes by committee, naming genetic diseases and conditions is quite haphazard. Often the physician who first identifies a pattern of signs and symptoms suggests a name, or the disease takes on the physician's name. Genes and genetic conditions are often named from the symptoms they cause, what the gene does, or who discovered the abnormal condition. In the case of cystic fibrosis, the phrase "cystic fibrosis of the pancreas" was first coined in 1938 by researcher Dorothy H. Andersen of Columbia University. Through her research, Anderson had recorded certain microscopic features she routinely saw in pancreatic tissues from infants and children who had died from a then-unknown disease. She named the disease cystic fibrosis based on her microscopic findings in the pan-

In a 2001 interview, Collins explained that the CFTR mutation causes an important protein to fold improperly. A parallel process may be illustrated through paper airplanes. Unless they are folded in a precise pattern, these toy planes cannot soar and loop through the air as they should. Collins hypothesized that in a mutated CFTR gene, if the gene's protein could be folded just right and returned to its normal place, the missing protein part (a specific amino acid

creas of cysts (sacs filled with fluid) and scar tissue (fibrosis) that replaced most of the normal pancreatic tissue. She also noted that infection of the lungs and damage to lung airways often appeared, as well. Andersen ultimately wrote a pioneering, comprehensive portrayal of the symptoms of CF and the changes it caused in organs.

Dr. Dorothy H. Andersen

Names also may originate from sources of basic elements of a disease or condition, such as sickle-cell anemia. Here, red blood cells take on a sickle-like appearance and can no longer transport oxygen normally throughout the body. A disease name also may originate from body parts affected by a disease or condition. For example, retinoblastoma describes where this disease occurs (in the eye's retina) and what it is (a blastoma, which is a cancerous tumor).

building block in the primary site of the protein called NBD1, which is part of the CFTR gene) may likely have only a mild effect that would not be enough cause CF.

In the interview, Collins said:

> The problem is it [the abnormally folded CFTR gene] gums up the works. Something about that particular [protein part] is supposed be right [at a specific location]. If it's not there, this complicated process of getting this whole thing assembled . . . gets hung up, and it doesn't finish the job. And parts of it that should have come together in a nicely formed, **globular** way get all strung out over the side, and it gets stuck in the machinery that is supposed to produce that protein in the right place at the right time, and it doesn't work.

The pathway to correcting the folding problem may eventually be found in current drug development, Collins said. Potential drugs might be developed to cushion the molecule and help it to fold correctly.

HOW IS THE CYSTIC FIBROSIS GENE INHERITED?

As discussed in Chapter 1, all humans inherit two CFTR genes—one from each parent. If one of the parents carries one damaged version of the CFTR gene and one healthy gene, and the other parent carries two healthy CFTR genes, their child cannot have the disease. This child will have at least one copy of the normal gene, but he or she will not develop the disease. If both parents, however, carry a mutated CFTR gene and the child inherits one copy of the damaged gene from each parent, the child will develop the disease. If the child inherits only one mutated CFTR gene from one of the parents, then he or she becomes a CF carrier. Additional combinations of the mutated CFTR gene from each of the two carrier parents can be passed on to their children in a variety of ways. The following discussion shows the pattern of inheritance in outline form (Figure 3.3).

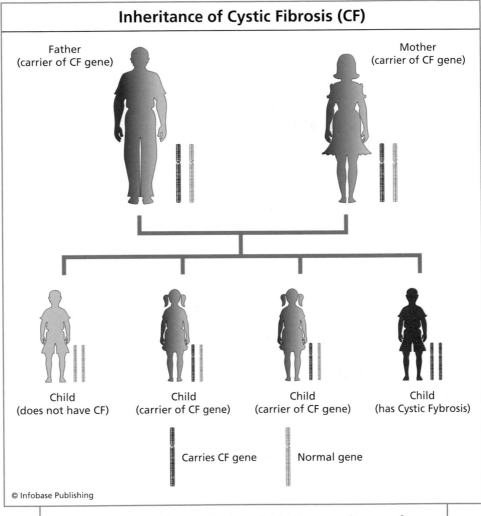

Inheritance of Cystic Fibrosis (CF)

Father
(carrier of CF gene)

Mother
(carrier of CF gene)

Child
(does not have CF)

Child
(carrier of CF gene)

Child
(carrier of CF gene)

Child
(has Cystic Fybrosis)

Carries CF gene   Normal gene

© Infobase Publishing

FIGURE 3.3 A mother and father who both carry the gene for cystic fibrosis have a one in four chance of having a child who has cystic fibrosis. There is a 50% chance the child will carry the gene, and a one in four chance the child will not carry the gene at all.

Two carrier parents of the mutated CFTR gene have a:

+ one in four chance of having a child with CF; this child will inherit both damaged CFTR genes from his or her parents.
+ one in four chance of having a completely normal child; this child will inherit only the two normal CFTR genes that his or her parents carry.

GENES AND CANCER

Cystic fibrosis is just one of many genetic diseases. Many cancers in CF patients appear about as often as they do in individuals without CF. Certain cancers, however, are significantly more common in patients with CF—digestive-tract and pancreatic cancers. Why this is so remains unknown, although many researchers suggest that genetic mutations or damaged structures in the digestive tract may be the culprits.

All cancers, or malignancies, begin with abnormal cells that multiply out of control. To date, researchers have identified genetic factors that show in various kinds of cancers, but definitive causes for cancer remain unknown. For example, scientists know that many cancers result from the interaction of a variety of factors, including genetic, environmental, lifestyle, and medical conditions.

As cancerous rogue cells rapidly increase in number, they can invade the human body and cause much harm. Cancerous tumors can grow, spread, and/or spin off malignant cells from primary tumors that then travel throughout the body. These loose cellular cannons may then damage and destroy other sites in the human body and also harm physiological processes, including blood cell production.

◆ two in four chance of having a healthy child, although that child will be a carrier of the CF gene; the child will also inherit a normal CFTR gene.

Yet chances are simply chances—a roll of genetic dice. When a mother's egg joins with a father's sperm to form a zygote (a fertilized egg), the resulting mix of genes is due to a genetically random event. Therefore, nothing is certain when two carrier parents have a child. The parents may instead have four noncarrier children, or perhaps three with CF, or maybe four carrier children—any combination that results from whatever random inheritance patterns are delivered during **fertilization**.

Families can carry the CF gene down the generations of their family trees. Prospective parents in families with histories of CF may choose to undergo genetic testing before planning a pregnancy. If both partners are carriers and the mother becomes pregnant, genetic testing can reveal whether or not the **embryo** is carrying one or both mutated CFTR genes. With today's sophisticated genetic testing methods, parents can obtain that information if they choose to do so.

4

SPOTLIGHT ON MOLECULAR BIOLOGY

Cells are the basic structural and functional units of every living thing (Figure 4.1). Literally trillions of cells make up the human body. Cells not only build the body's structure, they also convert nutrients from food into energy that the cell can use. Plants and animals, as well as simpler organisms like fungi, contain eukaryotic cells. A eukaryotic cell is any cell that has a nucleus and that contains organelles enclosed by a membrane. (An organelle is a part of a cell that performs a specialized task.) The second kind of cell is called a prokaryotic cell. It is a smaller, simpler type of cell found in bacteria. Its DNA is not located within a membrane-surrounded nucleus.

THE NUCLEUS: LIFE'S LINCHPIN

A cell's nucleus serves as the operations control center for issuing instructions for all cell processes. The nucleus also functions in transmitting the genetic information found in its DNA. This function of the nucleus is critical to maintaining life because the nucleus houses and protects the DNA. Protection derives from the double membrane (called the **nuclear envelope**) that encloses the nucleus and isolates it from the rest of the cell's main body and parts.

HOW DO CELLS WORK?

One might think that such a tiny bit of life would be constructed simply. Not so. As each organelle plays its part within the cell, all of their work makes for a busy, complex

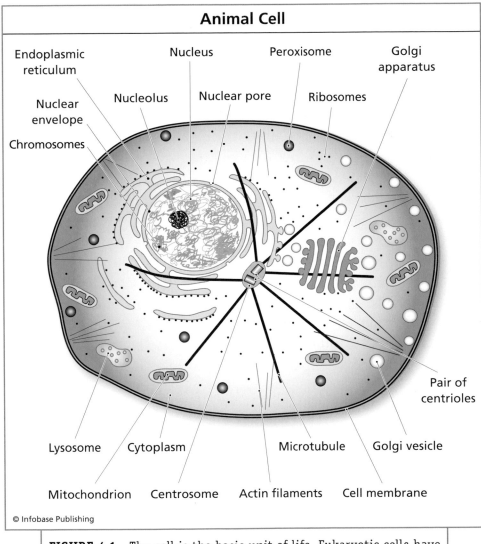

Animal Cell

Endoplasmic reticulum

Nucleus

Peroxisome

Golgi apparatus

Nuclear envelope

Nucleolus

Nuclear pore

Ribosomes

Chromosomes

Pair of centrioles

Lysosome   Cytoplasm

Microtubule   Golgi vesicle

Mitochondrion   Centrosome   Actin filaments   Cell membrane

FIGURE 4.1   The cell is the basic unit of life. Eukaryotic cells have a nucleus, in which most of the cell's genetic material is stored.

life system. Organelles are suspended within the cell's **cytoplasm**, a gelatin-like substance that fills the cell. **Ribosomes** are organelles that manufacture proteins by connecting amino acids according to the coded sequence on a strand of messenger RNA, which then takes over the protein-production process.

PROTEINS PLAY MANY PARTS

Proteins perform all of the tasks necessary for life to exist and to function. Proteins can be grouped into large areas of function, including:

- Antibodies, which bind to foreign matter such as viruses and bacteria to help protect the body from potential harm.
- Enzymes, which process nearly all of the countless chemical reactions that occur in cells.
- Messenger proteins, including some types of hormones, transmit signals among cells to manage life processes throughout cells, tissues, and organs. Growth hormone is a messenger protein, for example.
- Structural component proteins supply structure and maintenance of cell shape. These proteins are critical elements of body movement; one such example, actin, is part of cell structure and muscle tissue and takes part in muscle contraction.

Transport/storage proteins act like magnetic buses for atoms and small molecules inside cells. When needed, these proteins bind to targeted ions, molecules, or macromolecules and carry

WHEN GENES GO BAD

Genes carry out many complex functions and sometimes make mistakes. Think about electronic items: The more parts an electronic item has, the more chance there is that something will break down. Similarly, if something goes wrong during the protein production process, the resulting

them across **plasma** membranes for a variety of purposes. The normal CFTR gene is one example of a gene that produces a transport protein called the cystic fibrosis conductance regulator, or CFTR. This transport protein acts as a channel across cellular membranes that produce sweat, mucus, saliva, digestive enzymes, and tears. Called a chloride channel, it provides a way to allow free flow of chloride ions in and out of cells. (Chloride results from the chemical binding of chlorine with sodium.) The process helps control the water movement in tissues and is critical for production of normal mucus, which is a thin, watery, liquid-like secretion. On the other hand, the mutated CFTR gene that causes CF inhibits this water movement. That causes the formation of the thick, sticky mucus found in CF patients.

A normal CFTR gene's transport protein also serves to regulate operation of other cellular channels. This includes the channel that regulates the flow of sodium ions—positively charged sodium atoms—across cell membranes. The free flow of sodium ions across cell membranes is essential for healthy functioning of the lungs and pancreas. These organs become seriously damaged when the mutated CFTR gene causes those channels to malfunction.

damaged protein may express itself in a flawed fashion. The gene has become mutated. Although many protein mutations cause no damage, some of them can result in a variety of health problems.

What Are Chromosomes?

Genes and DNA live wrapped together in threadlike parcels inside a cell's nucleus. Each parcel is called a chromosome. DNA forms the chromosome before mitosis, the process whereby a cell divides itself into two identical cells. Chromosomes contain matching pairs of a single copy of a specific gene. People have 23 pairs of chromosomes (a total of 46). Forty-four of these chromosomes are known as autosomes, which are any chromosomes that are not sex chromosomes. Sex chromosomes are the other two that people carry; they determine gender. Each parent passes one sex chromosome on to their child. These chromosomes are either X or Y, and a pair of them determines a child's sex. Females have an XX pair in each of their sex chromosomes, so they can only pass on X sex chromosomes. The male's sex chromosomes each carry an X and a Y, which means the male sex chromosome passed on generally determines a child's sex.

Inheriting a genetic disease, abnormality, or trait involves two factors: the type of chromosome that carries the abnormal gene and whether the gene is dominant or recessive. In CF, the gene is located on chromosome 7, and it is a **recessive gene** (Figure 4.2). That means that a child must inherit two mutated CFTR genes (one from each parent), not just one, in order to have CF. In review, a child that inherits only one damaged CFTR gene does not have the disease but is a carrier of the mutated CFTR gene.

About 70% of the mutations seen in CF patients results from the deletion of three **base** pairs in CFTR's nucleotide sequence. The deletion triggers the loss of the amino acid phenylalanine, an essential amino acid that is one of many proteins that humans need. How much damage and where it occurs among the more than 900 possible mutations of the CFTR gene greatly determines the varying degrees of the illness. Some of the mutations may have little or no effect on CFTR function. Some may cause milder forms of the disease. And some trigger the full expression of the CF disease.

Other CFTR mutations can cause congenital bilateral aplasia of the vas deferens in males, which is incomplete or faulty development of the vas deferens. The vas deferens is a small, thick-walled tube that conveys sperm to the outside of the body as the ejaculatory duct. It is also called the

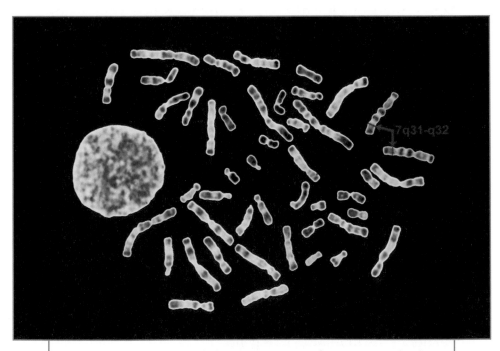

FIGURE 4.2 Mutation of the CTFR gene on chromosome 7 leads to the development of cystic fibrosis.

spermatic duct. The malformed or incomplete vas deferens in men with CF results in sterility because sperm cannot pass outside the body to fertilize a woman's egg. Surgical reconstruction can sometimes fix this problem and restore a man's fertility.

THE BASICS OF BASES

Each strand of DNA stores the specific genetic codes for building specific proteins. These protein codes are constructed from the four nitrogen bases of adenine (A), guanine (G), cytosine (C), and thymine (T). Scientists commonly use just the letters AGCT when referring to these bases. The sequence of these bases determines the particular genetic code for building specific proteins. These proteins are all highly specialized and will ultimately result in a living entity's particular genome, whether a plant, fish, bird, or human, to name a few examples.

THE DOUBLE HELIX

The nitrogen bases in DNA pair with another compatible base to form base pairs that are always the same. Specifically, A always pairs with T, and C always pairs with G. In other words, adenine and thymine chemically fit together, as do guanine and cytosine. Sugar and phosphate molecules then adhere to each base, forming the sides of the ladder and the three combined biomaterials (the base

FIGURE 4.3   *(opposite page)* The structure of DNA resembles a ladder. The nucleotides twist in a double helix, joined together by base pairs of nucleotides. The "rungs" of the "ladder" are made up of the base pairs.

DNA Structure

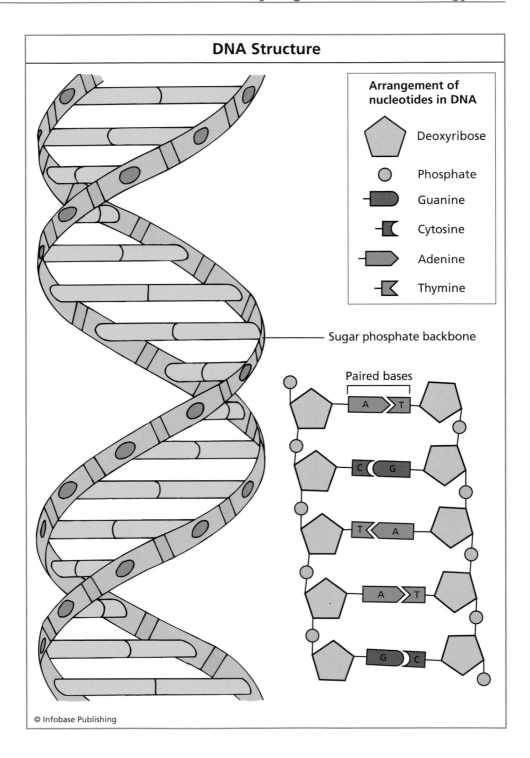

Arrangement of nucleotides in DNA

Deoxyribose

Phosphate

Guanine

Cytosine

Adenine

Thymine

Sugar phosphate backbone

Paired bases

A T

C G

T A

A T

G C

pair, the sugar, and the phosphate molecules) are called a nucleotide. Nucleotides form two long strings that coil around each other, giving the DNA molecule its spiraled

GENETIC TIME LINE OF DISCOVERY

The world of genetic study goes back more than 200 years. In 1859, Charles Darwin wrote his conclusion that natural selection (survival of the fittest) was the process that gave rise to and preserved a species' origin. Frederick Miescher, in 1869, isolated DNA from cells for the first time. In 1902, Walter Sutton's findings suggested that chromosomes were the keys to inheritance. Wilhelm Johannsen described the word *gene* as a unit of heredity in 1909.

A critical piece of research came in 1911 when Thomas Hunt Morgan and his students studied fruit flies, showing that the flies' chromosomes carried genes. Then in 1952, research by Alfred Hershey and Martha Chase showed strong support for the theory that genes are made of DNA.

A defining moment in genetics came in 1953, when Francis Crick and James Watson discovered that DNA aligned itself in a double helix structure. That finding turned the world of genetic research on its head. The structure was a copying mechanism for genetic material—the foundation of replicating all life forms. Until this discovery by Crick and Watson, scientific knowledge as to how DNA was passed from generation to generation was unknown. In 1962, both men received the Nobel Prize, along with Maurice Wilkins, who had done significant research into DNA.

The Nobel Foundation's recognition of the two men and Maurice Watkins remains controversial. Another DNA research scientist remained in the shadows, garnering no recognition configuration. This spiral shape, called a **double helix**, resembles a twisted ladder, with about 10 nucleotide pairs per turn of the helix (Figure 4.3).

for her pioneering work in DNA structure. In 1953, molecular biologist Rosalind Franklin had taken the first photograph that clearly showed the helical structure of DNA. She and Watkins had worked in the same laboratory in London, but a long-standing, contentious relationship prevented any cooperation between the two. Watkins refused to recognize Franklin as a scientific peer and instead treated her as a technical assistant. He also showed Franklin's DNA photograph to Watson. The picture confirmed the helical structure of DNA to both Crick and Watson, and they published those findings in *Nature* within weeks. Franklin received no global recognition. She died at age 37 from ovarian cancer.

Once the double-helix discovery was reported around the world, it proved a milestone in science history, revamping and modernizing the field of **molecular biology.** Scientists finally knew what DNA looked like. Since then, biological researchers have turned their attention to amassing wide-ranging, in-depth knowledge about many nuances of genetics. As scientists worked to understand how genes control the chemical processes within cells, that area of research quickly snowballed into an abundance of groundbreaking findings. Some of them include understanding the genetic code, how proteins synthesize, how to manipulate genes to create new drugs (i.e., genetic engineering), and how to determine the order of genes at extremely high speeds, a process called **gene sequencing.**

The double helix form of a DNA molecule is an elegant design. Hydrogen bonds connect the paired bases of A and T, then G and C. Because the four bases are not part of the backbone structure, they can occur in any order. That capability is highly significant because it opens up infinite possibilities for differing base sequences. Scientists studying the double helix structure have realized that this freedom in nature to mix base sequences means that the content of a DNA molecule offers infinite possibilities.

DECODING A GENOME

Gene sequencing is a process for identifying the nucleotide sequence in a piece of DNA. Nucleotides are one of the building blocks of DNA and RNA. They consist of a base of one of four chemicals (adenine, thymine, guanine, and cytosine) and one molecule respectively of sugar and phosphoric acid. Most genes contain a string of nucleotides arranged in a specific order that provides a code for producing a specific protein. A gene's code results from different combinations of three of the four nitrogen bases. These combinations are made from sets of three bases, such as TAG, TCA, and TGA, for example. A particular set of three consecutive bases tells an individual gene exactly which amino acids are necessary, and in what sequence, for the gene to build a specific protein. These sets of bases are called **codons**. The detailed sequences of specific nucleotides make up each individual's unique genetic code. Considered together, an individual's full genetic code is called a genome.

The ability of DNA to replicate itself is critical to life on Earth. By replicating itself, DNA can pass on its individual genetic material during cell division. That is possible because each strand of DNA in the double helix serves as a pattern for duplicating its own sequence of bases. The result? Every new cell now contains an exact copy of the DNA in the old cell.

TRANSCRIPTION AND TRANSLATION

Building all of the coded proteins that will eventually result in a specific life form involves two basic construction steps—**transcription** (Figure 4.4) and **translation**.

The first phase, called transcription, occurs when genetic information stored inside of a DNA molecule is converted into a comparable molecule called ribonucleic acid (RNA). RNA is used as a messenger of DNA's genetic information. It is single stranded rather than double stranded, like DNA. It can leave the nucleus, but DNA does not. The RNA holds the genetic information for building a specific protein. The RNA then transports its genetic information out of the nuclear envelope and into the cell's cytoplasm, where the protein will be made. Because of its transportation role in initiating protein production, RNA is called messenger RNA, or mRNA.

The next step is called translation. Once in the cell's cytoplasm, the mRNA intermingles with a ribosome to hand over the protein instructions. Recall that ribosomes are tiny organelles that are the sites of protein production in the cell's cytoplasm. Much as a building construction crew reads a blueprint to build a house, ribosomes follow a similar process. They first read the genetic code, and then arrange the specified amino acids (protein parts) in the precise order that the code calls for. By working with other crews—various enzymes—ribosomes make the final prescribed protein. A tiny piece of RNA called transfer RNA, or tRNA, moves a specific amino acid to the ribosomal site of

DNA Transcription

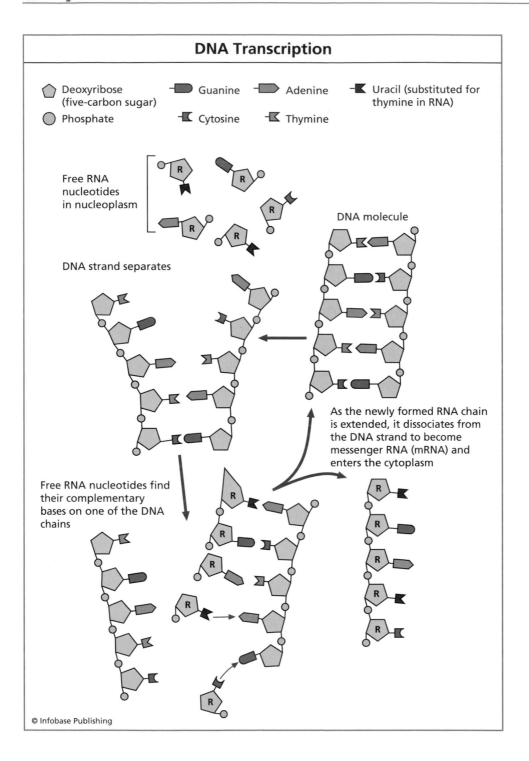

Deoxyribose (five-carbon sugar)

Phosphate

Guanine

Adenine

Uracil (substituted for thymine in RNA)

Cytosine

Thymine

Free RNA nucleotides in nucleoplasm

DNA molecule

DNA strand separates

As the newly formed RNA chain is extended, it dissociates from the DNA strand to become messenger RNA (mRNA) and enters the cytoplasm

Free RNA nucleotides find their complementary bases on one of the DNA chains a developing polypeptide chain. The entire DNA-to-protein process is called protein synthesis.

GENES EXPRESSING THEMSELVES

Recently, gene expression has generated much interest from molecular biologists and biotechnologists. Using a variety of techniques, researchers can manipulate DNA molecules to create new but artificial forms of DNA. The ability to make artificial DNA allows these scientists to dig for a deeper understanding of gene expression and manipulation. What is the artificial-DNA process? Usually researchers use a segment of one DNA molecule and combine it with a segment of another DNA molecule to create an entirely new sequence of DNA. The new DNA sequence is called recombinant DNA. Why is this kind of research important? Experts believe that the capability to manipulate DNA construction may eventually lead to new ways of preventing or curing genetic diseases, including CF and sickle-cell anemia, among many others. In fact, recombinant DNA pharmaceutical drugs that hold promise for treating or curing CF are already in various phases of clinical studies.

FIGURE 4.4 *(opposite page)* Transcription is the first step in DNA replication, wherein DNA copies itself to RNA.

MINING MORE GENETIC INFORMATION

Recall that the mutated CFTR gene that causes cystic fibrosis was discovered in 1989. During the 1990s, as new technologies became available to scientists, genetic research efforts quickly picked up pace. Much of the focus turned to cystic fibrosis, likely because CF involves a simple recessive gene and is the most common fatal genetic disease among Caucasian populations. Every year, about 1 in 3,000 babies are born with CF in the United States, although that incidence appears to be decreasing, according to some study results. Currently, about 30,000 children and adults in the United States and about 70,000 people worldwide have CF.

As one research team after another discovered new characteristics about the disease and the gene, knowledge about CF mushroomed. Other teams homed in on the chromosome location of the damaged CFTR gene. When scientists discovered that they could **clone**, or copy, both the normal and the mutated CFTR genes, that capability provided new DNA sources to work with. The ability to use a cloned mutated CFTR gene proved a powerful step forward. These clones have allowed researchers to conduct a variety of cell physiology experiments in order to understand cell functions better, including how cells grow and differentiate, how they transfer signals to other cells, and the role of cell function in neurological diseases, such as Alzheimer's disease, dementia, spinal paralysis.

THE BASICS

Why do researchers work to discover disease genes such as the mutated CFTR that causes cystic fibrosis? For one, detection of disease genes advances the understanding of the path of these inherited diseases. In addition, locating a disease gene can help improve medical diagnosis. It can also help identify specific genetic targets for further investigation. Studying specific genetic targets may lead to improved disease therapeutics, including the development of drugs that are specifically engineered to affect the genes that cause disease. Much research is underway by pharmaceutical companies to develop new drugs that will target precise areas in the human body, including mutated CFTR cells and cells of cancerous tumors. Cancer occurs when cells multiply out of control, and scientists want to find the keys inside cells that causes that to happen.

Analysis

Tracking down a disease gene first involves studying families that carry a disorder such as CF. Researchers gather data about the incidence of disease in family lines, in twins, and in people who have been adopted. Segregation analysis is one technique scientists use to search for a disease gene. In this method, researchers use genetic analysis to investigate any phenotype pattern—an observable physical and/ or internal characteristic—in a family line and compares it with a scientific, detailed model of inheritance patterns.

Genetic Markers

Before researchers can identify the gene responsible for an inherited disease, DNA markers show them the approximate location of the gene on the chromosome. A DNA marker is a specific gene that produces an easily identifiable genetic trait. The DNA marker is useful for studying family inheritance patterns and for analyzing large populations with a single genetic trait. As eggs or sperm are produced within

WHAT IS CHEMICAL GENOMICS?

Chemical genomics is a developing field that focuses on using organic chemicals called small molecules for exploration. It leads to production of chemical probes for in-depth research into protein and cell functions. The ultimate aim of chemical genomics is to translate the human genome at the molecular level. In the process, researchers will gain new biological insights that can eventually lead to new therapies. Libraries of useful small molecules (i.e., probes) are currently being built to streamline research. These repositories will allow scientists to home in quickly on specific probes that may prove useful in their particular research efforts. Probes play a multitude of roles in scientific research. A few examples include counting numbers of proteins in selected cells, tracing and tracking cell activities, and studying antibodies in depth. Uses for probes in science and biomedical research continue to expand.

Chemical genomics has proven extremely valuable to researchers. Although small molecules have been used for years in drug development, including manufacture of aspirin and antihistamines, it remains difficult for scientists to forecast which small-molecule compounds will be the most successful as a research tool for a specific project. Today's libraries contain female and male bodies, each person's 23 pairs of chromosomes within these cells exchange (or recombine) genetic material. If a specific gene of interest resides close to a DNA marker, the two will likely stay together in the recombination process. Remember, recombination is the exchange of pieces of DNA during sperm and egg formation. During the process, chromosomes randomly rearrange their genetic material, which increases the chances for genetic diversity.

thousands of small organic molecules that bring new efficiency to scientific searches. These libraries have been built largely under the sponsorship of the National Institutes of Health (NIH) and private sector companies. The NIH continues to develop its libraries with the goal of allowing biomedical researchers in the public sector to access chemical probes to study cellular pathways in increasing depth. In the private sector, companies have built libraries of their own probes that are specific to the company's research (e.g. pharmaceutical drug development companies). However, these are proprietary probe libraries, so no one outside the company can access the information.

The NIH Library initiative aims to help speed development of new drugs and agents that can detect and treat disease. This will enable researchers to provide early stage compounds that are made up of a wide range of unique targets and actions. Development of these libraries should also help in the discovery of small molecules needed for molecular imaging. Ultimately, the NIH hopes to aid doctors' efforts to acquire personalized profiles of cell and tissue function for each individual patient. Doing so will advance technologies to develop highly individualized ways to diagnose and treat people.

Thus, the gene and DNA marker will be passed on from parent to child. Markers are highly useful for tracking inheritance traits through generations of a family because the specific disease gene, such as CFTR, most likely lies near a specific marker.

Positional Cloning

The **positional cloning** method allows researchers to identify a gene exclusively by its location in the genome, and then to clone it. This technique is useful, for example, in identifying the CFTR gene.

The first step in postitional cloning is to conduct a **linkage study**, an experiment that searches out the genes and **genetic markers** that lie near each other on a chromosome. This is important because these genes cause two different traits, yet live close together on the chromosome. When genes are passed on to the next generation in a family line, the process tends to sweep these neighbors along with them as they divide and grow a new human being. Linkage helps lead researchers to a fairly accurate region on a chromosome where the disease-causing gene exists. Then, by **mapping** the linkage (often called genetic mapping), solid evidence appears that a disease transmitted from parent to child is linked to one or more genes. Genetic maps have been successful in detecting the single gene responsible for some inherited diseases, including CF and muscular dystrophy.

DNA SEQUENCING

DNA sequencing is a comprehensive description of the order of the bases in a selected stretch of DNA. The human genome comprises approximately 3 billion base pairs that make up DNA. Trying to fish around for a single gene among

ABOUT MICE, MEN, AND FRUIT FLIES

Studying the differences between mice and men goes back to the beginning of human civilization. Humans have been recording what they have observed in animal coat-color mutations for thousands of years, for example. The ancient Chinese made references to albino, yellow, and waltzing mice. By the 1700s, in China and Japan, numerous mouse varieties had been domesticated as pets. Europeans imported their favorites, breeding them with their local mice. In 1895, in Victorian England, "fancy" mice were highly esteemed and traded, and a National Mouse Club was formed. These mice had become a valuable form of entertainment and part of English social life.

The inbred local mice in England are the direct ancestors of today's hybridized laboratory mice. Work with mouse genetics gained ground in 1900, when Mendel's laws of inheritance prompted researchers to build mating programs to develop inbred strains of mice for study.

Until the early 1900s, gene researchers had no idea that the common fruit fly would prove to be a primary player in the genetics field. However, in 1911, an undergraduate researcher, Alfred Sturtevant, was studying these miniscule flies. He recognized that he was drowning in fruit fly data. He had gathered volumes of information before he realized that the amount of data he had was simply unmanageable. What to do? The only thing he could—map the locations of the fruit fly's genes. If he could do that, it would allow him to continue his work in an organized and systematic way. According to an old saying, necessity is the mother of invention, and for Alfred Sturtevant that was certainly the case. His mapping efforts paid off when he created the first map of fruit fly genes. That map allowed his

(continues)

(continued)

laboratory to continue its long-term project to track fruit fly mutations through generations.

Sturtevant's first gene map opened the door to new worlds of genetic study. Creating the first gene map can be compared to the 1947 invention of the electronic transistor by a research team at Bell Laboratories. As with Sturtevant's first gene map, the tiny, low-powered electronic device served as the first building block for today's electronic gadgets, such as the iPod and Blackberry, and the foundation for microchip and computer technology.

From the creation of Surtevant's first gene map onward, genetic studies moved along slowly. But in the late 1970s, the development of rDNA technology and the emergence of DNA sequence–based polymorphisms jump-started a groundswell of intense scientific interest and increased focus on genetic research. One seemingly simple outcome of using these two new technologies would later serve as another turning point in the field.

By combining the two technologies, scientists could distinguish the differences among the many strains of laboratory mice for the first time. In the past, this task had proved to be awkward, time-consuming, and ineffectual. The new capability provided genetic researchers with a much broader base of study targets and many more research options.

this immense DNA universe was once a daunting task. However, once DNA sequencing was developed, it became indispensable in tackling the job. Knowing the sequence of bases allows scientists to learn the kind of genetic information that a specific segment of DNA carries. Sequence information reveals which stretches of DNA contain genes. Scientists use that information to analyze those genes for any alterations in the sequence (that is, mutations) that may cause disease. Scientists continue working to expand and improve sequencing methods.

DNA sequencing is useful in revealing a mutated CFTR gene, because not all screening tests can find the gene. For example, blockage or nonexistence of the vas deferens in men occurs not only in CF but in other disorders as well, including some birth defects. Because the disease course in CF patients varies widely, a man may be unaware that he has CF until he experiences infertility. Because routine screening can miss finding a mutated CFTR gene, researchers have discovered that gene sequencing adds useful genetic details for double-checking a man's seemingly negative CF screening results.

TOOLS OF THE TRADE

Genetic knowledge advances as technology and research tools become increasingly sophisticated, as discussed above. All of the following technologies play invaluable roles in genetics studies:

- **DNA microchip technology**
- polymerase chain reaction
- restriction enzymes
- recombinant DNA
- **fluorescence in situ hybridization**

DNA Microchip Technology

Developing tests for a particular mutated gene is difficult. For one, most large genes have numerous areas where mutations occur. The damaged CFTR gene is one example. More than a thousand mutations can exist at various locations in the CFTR gene. DNA chip technology can easily identify these multiple mutations.

A DNA microchip is a miniature glass plate encased in plastic. Each chip holds thousands of short, synthetic, single-stranded DNA sequences that match the DNA in the normal gene under study. Researchers then study two blood samples. One sample comes from the person under study, and one is a control blood sample that carries no mutations in the CFTR gene. Denaturing the samples—that is, separating the two complementary DNA strands into single-stranded molecules—comes next. The long strands are cut into smaller pieces that are easier to work with. Each piece is then labeled by attaching a fluorescent dye. Green dye labels the person's DNA, and red dye labels the control (normal) DNA. Both pieces are then placed into the chip, where they bind to the synthetic DNA sequences that already have been placed on the chip. A person with no mutation for either gene will show both red and green samples bound to the DNA sequences on the chip. However, if the person does carry a CFTR mutation, the individual's DNA will bind incorrectly to its counterpart on the chip that holds the mutation. The region is then closely inspected to confirm that the mutation is indeed present.

Polymerase Chain Reaction (PCR)

Polymerase chain reaction is a fast, inexpensive way to copy small segments of DNA. Sometimes called molecular photocopying, PCR offers a way to study isolated pieces of DNA from the huge amounts of a DNA sample necessary for molecular and genetic analyses. The test is highly sensitive in measuring genetic expression, including that of the mutated CFTR gene. This sensitivity may provide a way to accurately measure the effects of new drugs and therapies now in clinical trials for treating people with CF.

Most gene mapping techniques rely on PCR. New advances in laboratory and clinical techniques use PCR to diagnose genetic diseases and disorders and to detect bacteria and viruses. PCR also helps with DNA fingerprinting. The technique is considered a giant step in advancing molecular biology largely because it allows researchers to produce millions of copies of a specific DNA sequence in about two hours. Therefore, research projects move forward much faster than they did before PCR became available. PCR's creator, Kary B. Mullis, received the Nobel Prize for Chemistry in 1993 for developing this procedure.

Restriction Enzymes

In the early 1970s, **restriction enzymes** became one of the tools that scientists used to manipulate DNA. Restriction enzymes identify and cut specified short sequences of DNA. The enzymes live in bacteria, where their job is to absorb any invading DNA. They are sometimes called molecular scissors because they can recognize a specific sequence of double-stranded DNA, and then cut the DNA at an exact site. These enzymes have proved to be a significantly useful tool for mapping genomes. Restriction enzymes are used in many areas of CF research, from studying variations of the bacteria that commonly cause lung infections in CF patients, to researching chloride channel properties.

Recombinant DNA

Recombinant DNA (rDNA) techniques are valuable in manipulating DNA molecules, which enables microbiologists to study gene expression. Recombinant DNA molecules are constructed outside of living cells by connecting natural or synthetic DNA segments to DNA molecules. These molecules can then replicate themselves inside a living cell. Molecules that result from **DNA replication** are also known as rDNA molecules. To simplify the concept of rDNA, these are DNA sequences in which the sequence from one microorganism recombines with an inserted DNA sequence from a plant, human, or animal. This results in a DNA sequence that shows the explicit modification that was programmed into it, thus exhibiting the highly specific modification. Using the rDNA process has resulted in scores of valuable medical substances. Two examples include the drug Pulmozyme, which helps ease breathing in CF patients, and the hepatitis B vaccine, which prevents often-debilitating inflammation of the liver. Hepatitis B is an infectious virus (often called HBV) that can seriously damage the liver. The disease is especially dangerous in CF patients because their livers are already injured.

Fluorescence In Situ Hybridization (FISH)

The FISH process allows researchers to visualize and map the genetic material in a person's cell, including specific genes or parts of genes. FISH increases scientists' ability to understand a variety of chromosomal abnormalities and other genetic mutations. It is often used for prenatal diagnosis of inherited chromosomal defects, including cystic fibrosis. The technology is used to identify exactly where a specific gene is located in a person's chromosomes. The FISH process consists of preparing short sequences of single-stranded DNA that match a part of the gene that the researcher wishes to study. These short sequences are probes, and they are labeled by attaching a colorful fluorescent dye. The dye then flags the location of the chromosome that is under scrutiny (Figure 5.1).

WHAT IS A TRANSCRIPTOME?

A **transcriptome** is a collection of all gene transcripts in a given cell. Unlike a genome—the complete DNA sequence of every life form—a transcriptome comprises an extremely small percentage of the genetic code that is transcribed

Fluorescence In Situ Hybridization

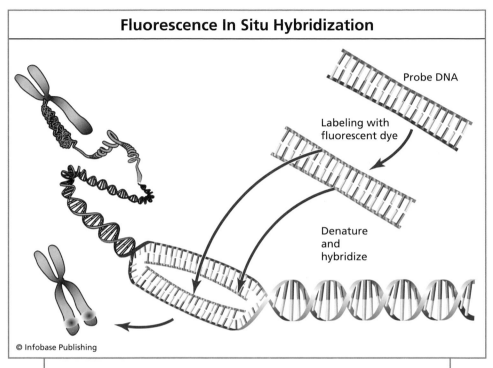

Probe DNA

Labeling with
fluorescent dye

Denature
and
hybridize

© Infobase Publishing

FIGURE 5.1   The FISH process allows scientists to further understand chromosomal abnormalities and other genetic mutations. The
fluorescent dye used on the probe DNA flags the location of the
chromosome in question.

into messenger RNA (mRNA)—about 5% or less in the
genome of humans and other mammals. Transcription
into mRNA is the required first step in building the specific
protein exactly as its genetic code instructs. Because the
sequences of mRNAs match the DNA sequences of the
genes from which transcription takes place, researchers
can discover when and where a gene is turned on or off in
many types of cells and tissues. Because most genes still
have no known function, searching a transcriptome data-
base offers scientists a list of all of the tissues in which a
gene is expressed. This knowledge provides clues to a particular gene's function.

A KNOCKOUT MOUSE FOR CYSTIC FIBROSIS

A **knockout mouse** is a mouse in which researchers inactivate (or knock out) an existing gene by using an artificial piece of DNA to replace it or disrupt its activity. In CF research, knocking out the mouse's own CFTR gene and replacing it with the mutated CFTR gene changes the mouse's phenotype in some way, which opens the door for researchers to explore any resulting clues about what the particular knockout gene normally does. Because human and mice genes are similar in many ways, whatever change occurs in a knockout mouse can yield useful information about human genes (Figure 5.2).

Mice strains created by knocking out the CFTR gene have helped to advance research into CF. Studies using a CFTR knockout mouse have shown that the illness results largely from the inability to clear specific bacteria from the lungs, which in turn triggers mucus retention. The mass of mucus left in the lungs provides a rich environment for bacterial growth, which causes the lung infections that occur repeatedly in CF patients. CFTR knockout mice have become **model organisms** for developing new options for working toward correcting the defective CFTR gene and eventually curing the disease. Knockout mice aid research into other genetic diseases, as well. Many different kinds of knockout mice have been created to facilitate research into an extensive list of diseases.

COMPARATIVE GENOMICS

With the vast amounts of data currently available about the human genome, scientists now have extremely powerful tools to study how genetic factors affect complex diseases, such as CF, cancer, diabetes, and cardiovascular disease. They also have detailed maps of genomes of a variety of

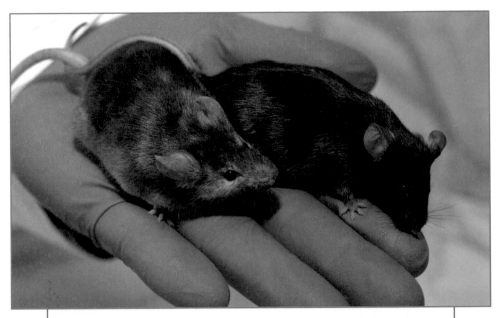

FIGURE 5.2   Knockout mice help scientists learn about particular genes. Scientists "knock out" a particular gene with an artificial piece of DNA and can learn more about what that gene normally does. The mouse on the left has had its hair growth gene knocked out.

animals and fungi. Each life form yields distinctive insights into human health and disease, and that potential has sparked a new field of biological research called **comparative genomics**. Here, researchers compare these varied genomes with the human genome to identify areas of differences and similarities. Comparative genomics offers scientists an increased ability to understand the structure and function of human genes in order to develop new ways to fight human disease. It is also a robust tool for studying evolutionary changes among differing life forms. That capability helps researchers pinpoint genes that are conserved among species, as well as genes that express each organism's varying characteristics. Computer-based analysis can then home in on the genomic features that have been preserved in a variety of organisms over millions of years. Doing so allows researchers to pin down the signals that control gene function and eventually help in discovering new and novel directions for treating human disease and improving health.

To date, this rapidly growing field of comparative genomics has already yielded results. A March 2000 study, for example, compared the genome of the fruit fly with the human genome and discovered that about 60% of genes are conserved between the fly and human genomes—i.e., the two life forms share a core set of genes. That genetic commonality allows researchers to use fruit flies for research that may have application in humans. Researchers have also discovered that two-thirds of the human genes known to play a role in cancer have counterpart genes in the fruit fly. In addition, scientists have inserted a human gene associated with early onset Parkinson's disease into fruit flies and discovered that the flies show similar symptoms to those in humans. Parkinson's disease is one of a group of human motor system disorders. Patients with Parkinson's experience tremor (or trembling) in the hands, arms, legs, jaw, and face; rigidity (stiffness) of the arms, legs, and trunk; slow movement (called bradykinesia); and impaired balance and coordination. Successfully creating fruit flies that carry the human gene associated with Parkinson's disease is an especially heartening discovery. This capability raises the possibility of creating new models of fruit flies for testing treatments that target Parkinson's disease.

GENOME-WIDE ASSOCIATION STUDIES

Genome-wide association studies are another new, indepth, and efficient way to unearth genetic variations associated with a particular disease. These studies take

WHAT WAS THE HUMAN GENOME PROJECT?

The Human Genome Project (HGP) was a natural continuation of genetics research that began in 1990. As new technologies emerged that allowed scientists to sequence genes quickly, the HGP was born. Conducted under the umbrella of the National Human Genome Research Institute (NHGRI) at the National Institutes of Health, the project aimed to sequence and map the entire human genome. The group comprised a broad, collaborative research consortium of scientists based worldwide. By 2000, HGP scientists had sequenced 90% of the complete sequence of all 3 billion base pairs in the human genome, and encountered surprises along the way. In 2001, the group published its first working draft of DNA sequencing in the journal *Nature*. Dr. Francis Collins, the director of NHGRI until 2008, explained the project's rationale: "It's a history book . . . a narrative of the journey of our species through time. It's a shop manual, with an incredibly detailed blueprint for building every human cell. And it's a transformative textbook of medicine, with insights that will give health care providers immense new powers to treat, prevent, and cure disease."

The project was complete in 2003, and the massive library of gene-sequencing information was made available to biomedical researchers worldwide.

Cystic fibrosis researchers have accessed deeper levels of understanding since the HGP was completed. They will continue to unlock mysterious, yet-unknown genetic knowledge from a new National Institutes of Health project, announced in January 2008. Named the 1,000 Genomes Project, its goal is to sequence and catalog DNA variations within the human genome at the

(continues)

(continued)

deepest level of detail possible. The 1,000 Genomes Project is made possible because of recent, fast-developing sciences of sequencing technology; **bioinformatics** (the use of computers to analyze biological data); and **population genomics** (the study of the role of genetic factors across groups of people). The genomes will be gathered from a thousand or more unidentified people from around the world.

Researchers have indicated that the results from the 1,000 Genomes Project should greatly streamline research into cystic fibrosis and many other genetically based conditions. Once completed, the project will greatly increase the sensitivity of disease discovery efforts. The new knowledge may dramatically change current medical practice by guiding the development of new drugs. It may also provide new ways to conduct genetic manipulation that could one day lead to prevention and cure of all genetic diseases, including cystic fibrosis.

a broad-brush approach to finding these differences by having researchers scan genetic markers across complete sets of human genomes. Once they discover new genetic associations, they can put the information to work in developing more efficient and effective ways to detect, treat, and prevent a specific disease. These kinds of studies are helpful in uncovering genetic variations that contribute to complex diseases, including CF, cancer, diabetes, asthma, heart disease, and mental illness. By using the information collected from these studies, researchers aim to build a foundation of gene associations that can someday serve the field of medicine in developing individualized, customized treatment strategies.

Genome-wide association studies are already paying off. In 2005, three independent research studies of macular degeneration (a condition of aging that causes blindness) linked a variation in the gene for complement factor H with expression of the eye disease. Complement factor H makes a protein that plays a role in regulating inflammation. Before this study, it was not a widely held belief that inflammation might make a significant contribution to this common eye disease.

HIGH-TECH TOOLS AND ADVANCING KNOWLEDGE

The new fields of comparative genomics and genome-wide association studies could not have emerged without the technology advances developed by the Human Genome Project and **HapMap**. The novel technologies that enable development of these new avenues of research include computerized databases that contain the reference human genome sequence, a map of human genetic variations, and a variety of new technologies that can rapidly and accurately analyze samples of whole genomes for genetic variations that play a part in genetic disorders.

CURRENT TREATMENTS FOR CYSTIC FIBROSIS

At this time, cystic fibrosis has no cure. Current treatments focus on keeping CF patients free of infection and as healthy as possible. CF therapies aim to lessen the amount of mucus in the lungs, control lung inflammation and infection, improve air flow in and out of breathing passages, prevent intestinal blockage, and maintain a high level of nutritional status and physical fitness.

Over the past decade, CF patients have benefited significantly from treatments that incorporate a blend of new and old therapies. Availability of newer antibiotics, mucus-thinning drugs, medical devices called **bronchodilators** that help loosen mucus from the lungs, and advancement in nutritional knowledge geared to CF patients' needs are a few recent developments that increase treatment effectiveness and quality of life. Treating CF patients with a blend of therapies tailored to fit each patient's needs has significantly increased the health and life expectancy of CF patients, according to the NIH Heart, Lung, and Blood Institute.

COPING WITH LUNG PROBLEMS

The two primary areas that cause lung problems include bacterial infection and mucus-clogged airways that obstruct breathing. Various therapies help treat these primary problems of CF. Highly effective drugs today include antibiotics, mucus-thinning and **anti-inflammatory medications**, high-dose vitamins, and replacement enzymes. In addition, physical therapy integrates modern tools combined with older lung-clearing techniques for higher success levels of loosening mucus. All of these contributions have added significantly to patients' health and comfort.

Bacterial Infection

As previously mentioned, the bacterial species *Pseudomonas aeruginosa* plays a primary role in causing the repeated lung infections that occur in CF (Figure 6.1). Other bacterial species also trigger such infections. For example, *Stenotrophomonas* bacteria are commonly found in mucus samples from CT patients. Less common bacterial species discovered in mucus samples include certain types of **anaerobes** and additional bacterial species.

Antibiotics are the most effective way to treat the ongoing low-grade lung infections that most CF patients endure. However, while antibiotics can decrease the frequency and severity of attacks, the disease-causing bacteria are never totally eradicated. The organisms left behind will flourish once again in the mucus that remains in the lungs. When the level of bacteria grows to a certain point (called a bacterial load), it will trigger another infection, and the infection-treatment cycle begins once more.

With the abundance of antibiotics available for treatment of lung infections, the choice of which medications to use depends on several factors: the exact strains of bacteria involved, the seriousness of the patient's condition, and the patient's history of antibiotic use. The drugs may be given orally for mild airway infections or **intravenously**, which is usually done for severe infections or when no oral

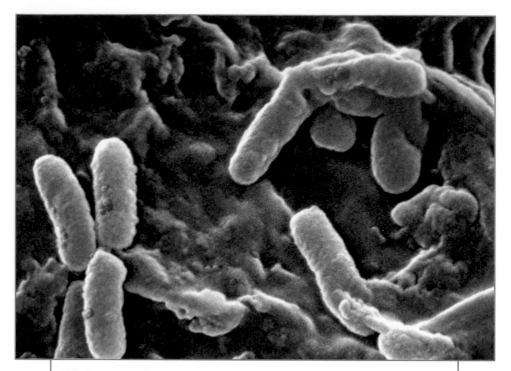

FIGURE 6.1   The bacteria *Pseudomonas aeruginosa* infects the lungs of cystic fibrosis patients, and can develop resistance to antibiotics.

antibiotics have worked. Another route of drug delivery is inhalation, which is a common way to administer medications to CF patients. Inhaling **aerosolized medications** is especially useful because the inhaled mist that contains the drug rapidly reaches airway targets (Figure 6.2).

Two commonly used drugs given through inhalation therapy include TOBI (tobramycin solution), an antibiotic, and the recombinant drug Pulmozyme (dornase alpha), a mucus-thinning medication. Studies have shown that Pulmozyme also reduces the number of lung infections and improves lung function. Although TOBI and Pulmozyme may be effective, they are also extremely expensive. Each costs up to to $10,000 per year for treatment, according to Columbia University Health Sciences studies.

New drugs for CF are currently in various stages of development. Drug companies charge high prices for patented drugs (such as TOBI and Pulmozyme) because they spend billions of dollars to research, develop, and conduct the costly clinical trials required by the U.S. Food and Drug Administration (FDA) in order to be marketed. Developing a new drug usually takes a decade or longer and can cost an estimated $1.5 billion. Patent laws protect drug formulas developed by pharmaceutical companies for a certain amount of time. That allows companies to be the only ones that can market their particular drugs, regain their financial investment, and profit from their efforts. But once a drug patent expires, other drug companies (or the same one that developed the drug) can make and market a cheaper generic form of the original drug. Generic drugs are exactly the same formula as the original drug and are less expensive, because by law they do not need to go through costly clinical trials. The company making the generic drug must only demonstrate to the FDA that their new product works the same as the formerly patented one.

Both TOBI and Pulmozyne are still protected under U.S. patent laws. No other company can make cheaper generic versions until the patents expire. TOBI's patent expires in 2014, which will open the door to other companies making generic versions of this medication. Pulmozyme, on the other hand, may never have a generic version. Pulmozyme is classified differently than drugs made from chemicals. It is classified as a biologic (or biopharmaceutical) drug, one that is made using live cells or organisms. As such, it is controlled under different laws than are conventional drugs. No laws are currently available that will allow manufacture of generic versions of biologic drugs.

Using antibiotics for a long time to treat lung infections has a downside, however. Taking them over and over

FIGURE 6.2 Many CF patients, including children, inhale medication for lung infections because aerosol drugs quickly reach airway targets.

increases the risk that drug-resistant strains of bacteria will develop in the lungs. This poses a serious barrier to treatment when conventional antibiotics no longer kill common bacterial strains. New ways to control infection must then be found, if possible. Researchers are developing promising new antibiotics that will offer innovative weapons in fighting resistant bacterial strains.

Other Medications

A wide range of medications are available today to reduce symptoms and complications of CF, as well as to slow the progression of the disease:

- *Steroids* are the most effective drugs for lessening lung inflammation resulting from repeated lung infections. Oral or inhalation delivery methods are available. Flovent (fluticasone propionate) and Pulmicort (budesonide) are two examples of drugs used to reduce inflammation.
- *Mucolytic drugs* help increase sputum volume and thin the mucus. These drugs, such as guaifenesin, DNase, and N-acetylcysteine, ease patients' efforts to cough up mucus and clear their airways.
- *Hypertonic saline* helps by chemically pulling more water into the airways, which adds a slippery quality to the airway linings that helps patients bring up mucus.
- *Bronchodilators* relax the bronchial muscles, allowing the airways to expand. A few examples include albuterol and Combivent (ipratropium bromide).
- *Ibuprofen*, an anti-inflammatory drug, slows the rate of decline of lung function in some people with CF.

◆ *Antibiotics* are abundantly available for treating lung infections. Some examples include ciprofloxacin, tobramycin, cephalexin, and azythromycin.

◆ *Human DNase* (dornase alpha) loosens mucus in the lungs. Here, researchers have found that DNase may also reduce the time a patient needs to spend in the hospital. Pulmozyme is an example of this type of drug.

Physical Therapy Techniques

These techniques work to dislodge the thick mucus and help the patient cough it up, ease breathing, and relieve

A TREATMENT PUZZLE

Several years ago, researchers discovered that a common antibiotic, azithromycin, can significantly improve lung function and support CF patients' health—but they could not figure out why. For years, azithromycin has treated middle ear infections and tonsillitis in children, as well as pneumonia in both children and adults. In 2005, the Cystic Fibrosis Foundation completed a six-month study of CF patients taking the drug. The study showed a 6% increase in lung function and an increase in weight. Also, the number of days a CF patient spent in the hospital to treat lung infections dropped by 47%.

One thing azithromycin cannot do is kill bacteria, such as the common *Pseudomonas aeruginosa* that causes CF lung infections. It is part of a group of antibiotics that do not kill bacteria, but inhibit bacterial growth. Many scientists think that the drug may reduce bacterial activity in CF patients, as well as lessen mucus thickness and loosen adherence of *Pseudomonas aeruginosa* in patients' airways. Research continues on how taking azithromycin works to benefit CF patients.

lung congestion. One of the oldest techniques used is called **postural drainage** (PD), also called chest physical therapy (CPT). Using PD along with specific breathing techniques has increased the effectiveness of this therapy. The method involves clapping or pounding the patient's chest and back as he or she leans over the edge of a bed. This helps free the sticky mucus from the lungs and airways so the patient can cough it up and spit it out. Sometimes PD can be applied with the patient sitting or lying prone. Sessions are often conducted three or four times daily and run from 20 to 30 minutes per session. Once the family or other caregivers learn the process, they can perform PD at home. Depending on a CF patient's level of lung congestion, PD may or may not become part of their daily care (Figure 6.4).

Undergoing PD can be uncomfortable for some people, however. Hanging over the side of a bed is awkward, and the caregiver's amount of force used to pound the patient's back may cause pain. To fill the need for comfort, several medical devices have been developed over recent years. The devices can help older children and adults perform PD by themselves.

These medical devices include:

◆ Electric chest clappers (often called mechanical percussors)
◆ Inflatable vests that use high-frequency waves to force out the mucus vigorously
◆ Flutter devices, small handheld machines that patients breathe in and out of that trigger vibrations and dislodge the mucus
◆ Positive expiratory pressure masks, or PEPs, that vibrate to help break the mucus loose

Breathing techniques can also increase the effectiveness of clearing out mucus. One method is called forced expiration technique (FET). Here, the patient forces out a few breaths (called huffs), then changes into a relaxed breathing pattern. Another technique, called active cycle breathing (ACB), involves combining FET with deep breathing exercises to expand the chest and loosen secretions in the **bronchi**, the tubes leading from the trachea (windpipe) to the lungs; the bronchi provide the branching routes by which air passes into the lungs.

If the above therapies do not clear the airways enough, a patient cannot take in enough oxygen, and their blood oxygen level may sink too low. Oxygen therapy is then used to add oxygen to the blood. Oxygen is usually delivered through a mask or through nasal prongs that lie just inside the nasal openings (called nares).

Lung Transplantation

Removing a CF patient's damaged lungs and replacing them with healthy ones from a donor is one of the final options for treating end-stage lung disease. Transplantation is an important consideration because lung disease eventually kills almost all CF patients. The primary goal of transplantation is to improve the patient's quality of life. Since 1991, nearly 1,600 people in the United States with CF have received lung transplants. Recent studies show that life spans often increase in adults with CF who have had successful lung transplants, and many experienced dramatic improvements in their quality of life. In children, however, lung transplantation studies show mixed results. Although some children may live longer, most do not. Many children's bodies reject the transplants because they are physically too small to survive the large doses of powerful anti-rejection drugs required to overcome their body's natural immune response to reject the foreign lung tissue. Other children receiving lung transplants have died from different side effects, including kidney problems, tumor growths that resemble

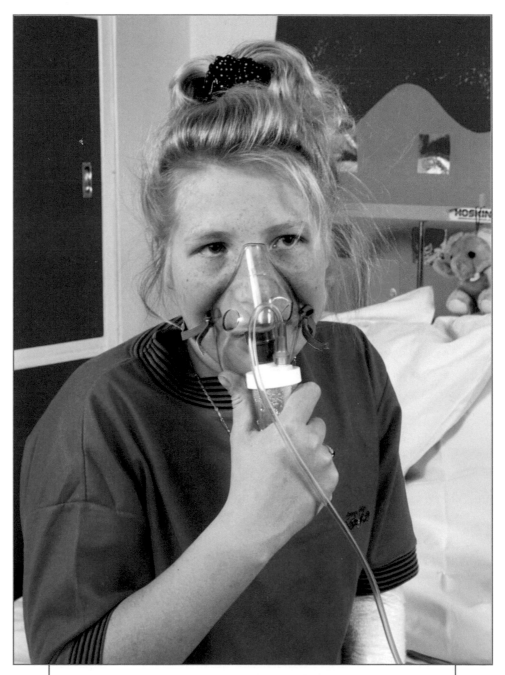

FIGURE 6.3   This CF patient is using a nebulizer, which administers her medication in a fine mist to target and loosen mucus in her lungs and airways.

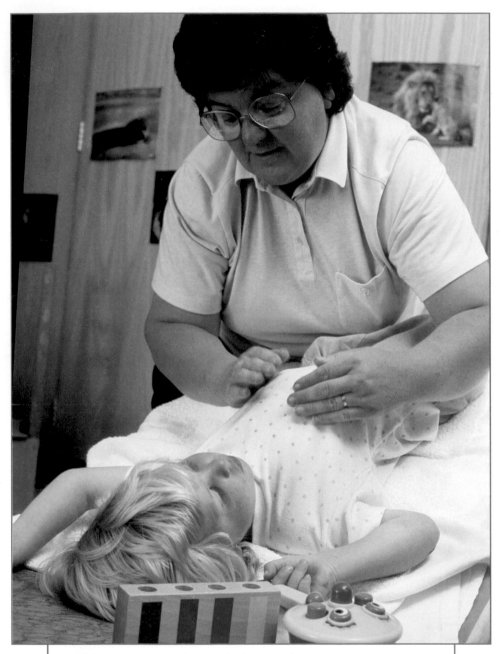

FIGURE 6.4 Certain kinds of physical therapy can aid CF treatment. Here, a physiotherapist administers postural drainage procedures to a young patient in a reclining position.

cancer, and infection. Because of the poor survival rates in children receiving new lungs, many physicians question the efficacy of doing these transplants in children at all.

But progress in survival rates appears to be improving. New study results from Columbia University Medical Center's Morgan Stanley Children's Hospital of New York–Presbyterian, released in March 2008, showed increased survival rates in CF children undergoing lung transplantation at their facility. According to the press release, the hospital claims a one-year survival rate of 96%, compared to national data that show a one-year survival rate of 83%. The facility's three-year survival rate is 90%, whereas national data for this time period is 67%. The Morgan Stanley unit attributes their increased survival rates to early detection of genetic signals of impending lung rejection. As soon as these signals appear, the transplantation team increases immunosuppression treatment.

Yet, immunosuppression agents can cause severe side effects, including osteoporosis (thinning of bones), obesity, growth of body hair or hair loss, and extreme growth of the gums (called gingival overgrowth), which can lead to mouth infections and teeth displacement. So the team must reach a balance of treating the patient with enough immunosuppression to curb rejection episodes, yet minimize the complications from these immunosuppression agents. Also, certain therapies now in development may eventually make the need for anti-rejection (i.e., immunosuppression) drugs obsolete. This offers future promise for helping children and adults survive lung transplantation and the years following the surgery.

History of Transplantation

In 1983, at the University of Pittsburgh, a surgical team performed the first lung transplant for CF. That inaugural procedure was performed as a combined heart-lung transplantation. The rationale for this pioneering effort was to avoid tracheal complications, while conserving the donor's healthy organs. The idea was to increase the availability of healthy organs. That meant that this CF patient received a heart-lung transplant from the still-viable organs of a **cadaver**. The transplant recipient then donated his or her healthy heart to someone with critical heart disease who needed a new heart.

While the exchange process seemed wise at the time, researchers soon discovered that the process added increased levels of risk to the CF patient. The patient already had a healthy heart. Therefore, undergoing an unnecessary heart transplant added increased risk for complications and offered no health benefits to the CF patient, compared to the benefits gained by only receiving two healthy lungs.

Since then, organ transplantation as a whole has made significant strides. Increasingly sophisticated surgical tools and techniques, better medications, and improved patient selection have all boosted postsurgical survival rates and added quality-of-life benefits for a transplant survivor. In 2007, for example, the University of Virginia (UV) announced a significant increase in survival rates of their lung transplant patients. (Not all were CF patients, though.) By 2005, the university's one-year survival rate for lung transplant patients was 98.08%, compared to the nationwide one-year survival rate of 87.6%, according to UV information. Today, Cystic Fibrosis Foundation data shows that about 50% of all U.S.-based transplant patients survive at least five years.

Selecting appropriate patients for lung transplantation is important for increasing the chances for postoperative success. Three primary factors are considered in selecting a patient for the surgery. These include the severity of breathing problems, life-threatening lung complications, and/or increasing resistance to the antibiotics used to treat the patient's lung infections. Also, the person's overall health and lifestyle are evaluated. Because CF affects both lungs, both of them need to be replaced. Once a patient is selected for transplantation, he or she must then wait until two healthy donor lungs become available.

Over time, extensive waiting lists of lung transplant–approved patients became an increasingly inefficient process for choosing a patient when healthy donor lungs became available. Unless a CF patient was near the top of the waiting list, they had to wait even longer. These very ill people often had to wait anywhere from a few weeks to several years to make their way up the list. Many died waiting.

But in 2005, waiting lists were abolished and a new system put into place. Now, all CF patients over age 12 who have been selected for lung transplants are regularly assessed to evaluate how sick they are and the chances they have for staying healthy after the transplant. The policy change works to ensure that available donor lungs are given to the patients who need them most and who will likely survive to benefit from them.

In the United States, about 900 lung transplants are performed every year, according to the Cystic Fibrosis Foundation. Since 1991, almost 1,600 people with CF have received lung transplants. An ongoing shortage of donor organs continues to plague the ability to give healthy lungs to all qualified patients.

Though the outlook for survival has increased since the first heart-lung transplantation in 1983, the procedure in children with CF remains risky. Adding years to a lung receiver's life is not a goal of transplantation. Improving the quality of life is the goal. Choosing to undergo a lung transplant is a difficult decision for CF patients and their families. Experts advise that patients take time to consider carefully all facets of possible outcomes. Receiving counseling from the patient's CF care team can help the person explore options, consider the risks, and discuss any other concerns.

Yet, the high cost of organ transplantation puts the procedure out of reach for many CF patients. According to studies done at Emory University, the cost of a lung transplant can range from $100,000 to $200,000. The lifetime cost of care for a lung-transplant patient is about $450,000, according to Washington University and the University of Pittsburgh.

Nutritional Needs

Dietary management is important for CF patients because of their inability to digest adequate nutrients. They lack the pancreatic enzymes that break down fat, starch, and proteins. Levels of the fat-soluble vitamins A, D, E, and K are often too low because the lack of enzymes prevents fats from breaking down and allowing these vitamins to change into useful nutrients. These unused nutrients leave the body, which leads to malnourishment.

Nutritional planning with the help of a doctor or skilled dietician can be customized so that each patient receives enough nourishment to support maximum growth and health. Higher-than-normal doses of vitamins A, D, E, and K are often prescribed, and enzyme supplements are commonly used to replace the missing pancreatic enzymes. In fact, nearly 90% of CF patients benefit from taking enzyme supplements before each meal and snack, according to CF specialists at the University of Arkansas for Medical Sciences.

Nutritional changes can aid in lessening the digestive problems that CF patients often experience. With CF, a patient's stools may become bulky, which makes bowel movements difficult and may lead to intestinal complications. Excess gas, bloating, and stomach pain may indicate constipation. Feces can sometimes build up inside the intestine and completely block their passage. This is a serious condition called **bowel obstruction**. Treatment for this condition involves inserting a tube directly into the stomach or intestine to relieve abdominal distention (swelling) and vomiting. If that maneuver fails to solve the problem, surgery may be necessary to remove the obstruction and restore normal intestinal function. Nutritional therapy to address digestive problems focuses largely on eating a well-balanced, high-calorie diet that is abundant in protein and carbohydrates and high in fat (to add to caloric intake). Taking oral pancreatic enzymes helps patients digest fats and proteins and absorb vitamins better. Mucus-thinning drugs can help prevent and treat bowel obstruction, as can enemas. Drugs that reduce stomach acid can help increase the therapeutic value of taking oral pancreatic enzymes, as well.

Sometimes a person with CF cannot eat enough calories to maintain or gain weight. To add nutrition and calories, the doctor may recommend administering a liquid formula through a feeding tube that goes directly into the intestine or stomach. The liquid formula feeds the patient during sleep in order to add to the day's calorie intake. Several options are available for feeding tubes:

- A nasogastric tube is passed every night through the nose and down the throat into the stomach.
- A gastronomy tube is surgically inserted through upper abdominal skin and directly into the stomach.
- A jejunostomy tube is surgically inserted into an area of the intestine to protect against gastric reflux.

Exercise

Participating in aerobic exercise is very important for children and adults with CF. The deep, rapid breathing rhythms reached through aerobic exercise helps loosen mucus and encourage coughing to bring it up and ease breathing. Also, by loosening airway mucus before a chest therapy session, the patient will maximize the benefits of the session. Consistent exercise also strengthens muscles (including chest

CYSTIC FIBROSIS CARE CENTERS

Patients and their families can find a rich resource for CF care and counseling at one of the more than 115 CF care centers accredited by the Cystic Fibrosis Foundation. The foundation also accredits 95 adult care programs and 50 affiliate programs nationwide. Care centers are located at community and teaching hospitals. Here, patients and families can access diagnoses, treatments, individual care, and counseling information. Nutritional, pulmonary (the respiratory system), and gastroenterological (the digestive system) expertise are also accessible at these centers. Psychosocial specialists are available to help patients make informed care choices and cope with their individual needs as they live with CF. That may include help with workplace issues, educational options, mental health concerns, and many other matters.

Founded by a group of parents in 1955, the Cystic Fibrosis Foundation is a nonprofit organization completely funded by donors. The mission of the foundation is to ensure development of new therapies for curing and controlling the disease. With headquarters located in Bethesda, Maryland, the foundation currently has 80 chapters and branch offices across the United States. The Cystic Fibrosis Foundation invests heavily in research, care, and educational programs. Research programs focus on basic genetic research involving the mutated CFTR gene and the development of treatments and therapies muscles), increases endurance and flexibility, and builds physical fitness, which is important when living with a chronic disease like CF.

Adults, adolescents, and children with CF can participate in any activity they enjoy that is safe and fits within their

for CF. Ultimately, the foundation's research efforts aim to find a cure for CF or a way to prevent the disease. As of November 2008, some of the potential CF therapies in development include gene therapy, protein repair therapies, ways to restore salt transport, and treatment for mucus problems. Current drugs in development span a broad range of therapies. These include anti-inflammatory drugs, medicines that will fight or prevent infections, transplant drugs, and development of highly effective nutritional supplements.

The foundation also actively supports educational programs for increasing awareness and understanding of CF. Programs focus on educational activities for schoolchildren, community and business leaders, laypeople, and professionals (including physicians, medical students, nurses, and other professional caregivers). Fund-raising to support these programs and continue foundation development is an ongoing effort. Fund-raising events take place continually across the country, usually planned and operated by local CF chapters. Outreach efforts comprise national press and broadcast coverage, involving famous people (such as baseball Hall of Famer Mike Schmidt and NASCAR driver Denny Hamlin) in fund-raising efforts, and sponsoring an annual CF conference in Williamsburg, Virginia. At this conference, CF researchers discuss their projects in front of an audience of scientists from academia and industry.

physical abilities. For example, adults and teens may enjoy running, swimming, dancing, working out in a gym, and playing sports. Children usually like any activity that involves high-energy output. These might include:

- ◆ running
- ◆ participating in sports such soccer and basketball
- ◆ jumping on a trampoline
- ◆ playing tag
- ◆ catching a ball

Whatever activities a person with CF chooses, it is important to be consistent. According to the University of Arkansas for Medical Sciences, CF patients should exercise aerobically for 30 to 60 minutes a day, preferably right before chest therapy to maximize the benefits of this treatment.

Treatment Roundup

For many years, CF patients did not survive infancy. For those patients who are diagnosed with CF after age 13, the prognosis is usually much better. This is because these people have not shown symptoms of CF until they have reached an older age. Studies show that these patients have milder lung disease, less pancreatic damage, and different CF mutations. People diagnosed later in life also have a better chance of living longer and more comfortably than infants and children who show clear symptoms early in life.

By the 1980s, new drugs and technologies had advanced enough to help many young patients survive into childhood or adolescence, according to the NIH National Heart, Lung, and Blood Institute. And with today's advancing treatment tools and therapeutics, many CF patients live to age 40 and beyond.

7

CURRENT RESEARCH OFFERS HOPE

Discovery efforts in cystic fibrosis include research that focuses on a variety of cutting-edge technologies. Gene therapy, nanotechnology, pharmacogenomics, and the use of rDNA are actively being studied for development of possible CF therapies.

WHAT IS GENE THERAPY?

Gene therapy is a way to fix or replace defective genes responsible for diseases such as CF. It involves a recombinant DNA process whereby cells are taken from a patient and altered by adding genes. These altered genes are then put back into the patient to provide the genetic codes for proteins that the patient lacks. Gene therapy involves using various techniques to replace damaged genes with healthy ones, correct defective genes, or fix a gene's malfunctioning protein. The goal is to treat or, eventually, prevent disease and other conditions. An abundance of research into CF therapies that uses gene therapy techniques is currently underway.

Ever since the 1989 discovery of the mutated CFTR gene, researchers have been seeking ways to transport a normal copy of the CFTR gene into the lungs and airways to replace the defective CFTR gene. Although many methods show initial promise in laboratory experiments using small animals, the results of clinical trials conducted using primate models and human patients have been disheartening. Scientists have yet to find a useful therapeutic method that is sustainable and repeatable.

In 1990, scientists successfully fixed mutated CFTR genes by adding normal copies of the CFTR gene to cell cultures in the laboratory. Then, in 1993, a patient received the first experimental gene therapy treatment. In this case, researchers changed a common cold virus to be a **vector** for carrying normal CFTR genes to the damaged CFTR genes in the lung's airways. However, the experiment proved unsuccessful because the normal CFTR gene randomly inserted itself into the patient's DNA—a problem that researchers are still trying to surmount. To date, lung cells have been used in CF gene therapy experiments. Lung cells are easy to gather, and lung damage is the primary life-threatening problem that CF patients face. Gene therapy is still used only in research. Until researchers can control where the healthy gene will insert itself into a patient's DNA, successful gene therapy for CF cannot be accomplished. Other barriers to gene therapy for CF and other diseases include problems of sustaining treatment benefits as cells reproduce and die, and overcoming immune reactions in patients.

Early gene therapy experiments highlighted the need for further investigation. Researchers must first find the most effective vector for transporting normal CFTR genes in order to develop useful treatments. Also, additional work must be done to establish the life span of treated lung cells, to discover the parent cells that produce CFTR cells, and to determine how long gene treatment should last. Researchers also must pinpoint how often the gene therapy needs to be repeated. Much work remains to be done.

Today, developing new CF drugs is an area of gene therapy research that is being widely studied. In one effort, scientists have finished a genetic map of the *Pseudomonas aeruginosa* bacterium, the most common cause of lung infections in CF patients. This genetic map provides a valuable resource for developing novel drugs that can specifically treat *Pseudomonas aeruginosa* infections.

Other researchers are looking for ways to break into the membranes of permanent colonies of *Pseudomonas aeruginosa* that live in the lungs. One recent study used an FDA-approved drug, Gallium, for this purpose. This metallic element resembles iron. Iron is necessary for the growth of these bacterial colonies, and the colonies misidentified gallium as iron. The bacteria began absorbing the gallium into their core centers. Like medieval knights breaking through castles to fight their enemies, the absorbed gallium proceeded to effectively kill the *Pseudomonas aeruginosa* colonies from the inside.

Although gene therapy holds promise, all the work to date remains experimental. No gene therapy has been identified as the sole factor in curing a specific disease, nor has the FDA approved any human gene therapy product for sale. The field has experienced some setbacks over the years, including the death of an 18-year-old in a 1999 gene therapy trial in an effort to treat his rare metabolic disorder. His death sparked widespread debate about the ethics involved in gene therapy and the need for increased oversight from FDA regulators to ensure the safety of the procedure in future gene therapy experiments. Despite these and other problems, scientists have gained ground in many aspects of gene therapy. Significant progress has been made in developing various gene transfer vehicles that transport healthy genetic matter to a targeted or general area within the body. Unlike early transport systems, today's vehicles are less toxic, increasingly efficient, and do not trigger an immune response in the patient—all significant strides that have helped move the gene therapy process forward.

A CLOSE-UP LOOK AT DRUG DEVELOPMENT

The Cystic Fibrosis Foundation underwrites many research efforts. Their current drug research pipeline includes two therapies that have already gained FDA approval and are in use—Pulmozyme and hypertonic saline. Both thin mucus to help ease breathing. Two anti-inflammatory drugs are already available. TOBI and azythromycin work to reduce inflammation of the airways, and many CF patients currently use them. Also, one gene therapy drug is in preclinical stages. Other categories of drugs under study include those that:

- Either help lessen the effects of the mutated CFTR gene or repair the damage inside the gene
- Restore salt transport
- Decrease inflammation
- Fight infections
- Support lung transplantation
- Increase nutritional status

A close-up look at some of the drug therapies in development offers a few more details about the methods used and their outcomes. The following three therapies show the most promise for dealing with CF: compacted DNA, therapeutic DNA carriers, and hypertonic saline.

Vectors

Most gene therapies involve transporting genetic material inside of a living genome, such as a lab mouse or bacterium. Transport systems, called vectors, are most commonly created from specific viruses that have been genetically engineered to carry normal human DNA. However, using viruses

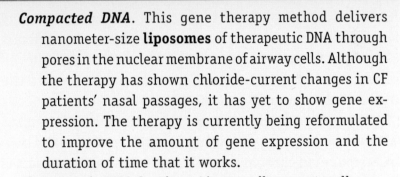

Compacted DNA. This gene therapy method delivers nanometer-size **liposomes** of therapeutic DNA through pores in the nuclear membrane of airway cells. Although the therapy has shown chloride-current changes in CF patients' nasal passages, it has yet to show gene expression. The therapy is currently being reformulated to improve the amount of gene expression and the duration of time that it works.

Therapeutic DNA Carriers. Airway cells are naturally covered with a mucus barrier, which impedes gene delivery into cells. Work is underway to create nanoparticle carriers that contain recognition and binding features that will allow them to surmount this mucus barrier and directly attach therapeutic genes to lung cells.

Hypertonic Saline. Inhaling this water-based concentrated salt solution may provide long-term benefits for lung health in CF patients. One study involved a group of 24 adolescent and older patients with CF who inhaled a hypertonic saline solution four times a day for 14 days. Results showed that this simple, inexpensive treatment significantly improved mucus clearance and lung function, thereby reducing breathing problems.

as vectors is a two-edged sword. Why? Because viruses effectively encapsulate and deliver their own genes directly into a cell, thus triggering a disease. To keep this from happening, scientists have been working to keep the good viral functions—encapsulating and delivering material directly into a cell—while knocking out the disease-causing elements of these viruses by manipulating the virus's genome (Figure 7.1).

The altered viruses are then loaded with genetic materials that contain therapeutic human genes. Once researchers have chosen target cells, such as damaged lung cells from CF, they then "infect" those target cells with the genetically loaded viral vector. Inside a target cell, the vector unloads its therapeutic-gene cargo, which then aims to spur development of a healthy, functional protein that can return the target cell to its normal condition.

Other gene-delivery systems have been developed, as well. One of the new synthetic vectors is an artificially constructed human chromosome 47. As a transport system, it is more like a big bus than a tiny car. This big-bus vector carries huge quantities of genetic code, but because of its size, it has difficulty passing through cellular membranes and into the nucleus of a target cell. Work continues to advance the effectiveness of this type of vector.

Liposome vectors are just the opposite. These spherical vesicles made from lipids (fats) easily pass through cell membranes because both the vector and the cell contain the same kind of membranes. That allows liposome vectors to fuse with the cell's membranes and deliver its DNA load. Liposomes internalize whatever media they are created in. By making them in a DNA solution, they become DNA deliverers. All of these gene-delivery systems remain in the early research stages to test their safety and usefulness.

Once a therapy gene has been inserted into a cell, a key goal toward attaining successful gene therapy is being able to tightly control the level of the gene's on-off functions. This is because during gene therapy, the ability to regulate gene expression consistently—and precisely when it is

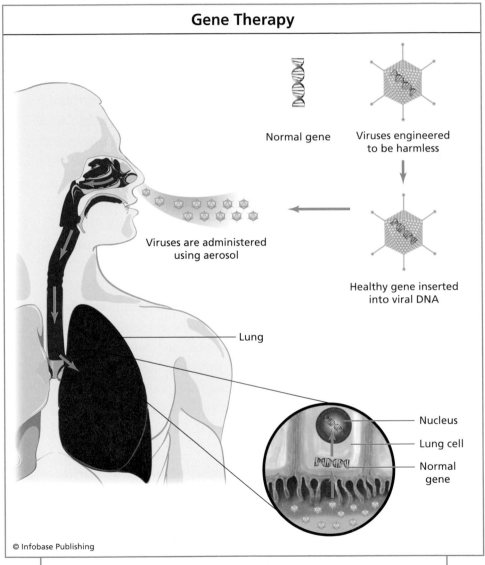

Gene Therapy

Normal gene

Viruses engineered to be harmless

Viruses are administered using aerosol

Healthy gene inserted into viral DNA

Lung

Nucleus

Lung cell

Normal gene

© Infobase Publishing

FIGURE 7.1 In some forms of gene therapy, a virus that has been genetically engineered to be harmless is used to deliver healthy genes to the cells of a patient.

needed—then shut off its expression when the therapy is completed, is critical to managing the gene delivery process effectively and safely. Research continues into the switching functions of gene expression.

PHARMACOGENOMICS

This emerging field combines the "pharma" from *pharmacology* and the "genomics" from the study of genetics. Researchers use **pharmacogenomics** to study how an individual's unique genome affects his or her particular response to a drug therapy. The goal is to someday develop customized drugs that will be adapted to each person's unique genetic makeup. This task will involve pharmaceutical companies who will develop drugs based on the exact proteins, enzymes, and RNA molecules linked to genes and diseases. Companies could then produce therapies that will accurately target specific diseases. That specificity will likely maximize the drug's therapeutic effects while avoiding damage to healthy cells in the area. Developing these specialized drugs will eventually allow doctors to prescribe the best treatment for patients during their first visit because the drug of choice will be based on the patient's own genetic profile.

But as a field in its infancy, pharmacogenomics must surmount certain barriers before the science can be widely used. A few obstacles include:

◆ Overcoming the complexity of locating gene variations that will affect a drug's response
◆ Expanding drug alternatives so that patients who cannot use the few available drugs are not abandoned without treatment options
◆ Convincing pharmaceutical companies to agree and find funding to conduct this kind of costly

drug development that will likely serve only a small segment of the population

◆ Reeducating health-care providers in a much more complex process of prescribing and administering drugs than is used today.

NANOTECHNOLOGY

What is **nanotechnology**? It is a new scientific field where scientists aim to build devices at atomic or molecular scales. How small are these scales? A nanometer is one billionth of a meter, or about $^1/_{50,000}$ of a single human hair, according to the Massachusetts Institute of Technology and many other nanoresearch centers.

Nanomedicine is one area of nanotechnology where novel medical research is taking place. Until the birth of nanomedicine, scientists were unable to thoroughly catalog all cells, cell parts, and the molecules within those cell parts. Today, by using extremely high-powered microscopes and other visualization tools, scientists can study and categorize cellular parts and subparts. The primary goal of today's nanomedicine research is to completely and reliably quantify and catalog each cell and cell part, down to their molecular and atomic levels. This information will offer new insights into how molecular mechanisms work. Once the interactions among and within all human molecules are completely cataloged, researchers can look for biological patterns and relationships. By mapping these networking systems and watching how they change over time, scientists will amass a complex view of the natural order and rules of biological design.

Early research already shows that drugs can be linked to nanocarriers that are specific for certain cells and organs. Eventually, scientists aim to:

◆ Cure disease at the molecular level
◆ Build synthetic biological devices, such as tiny implantable pumps, for drug delivery
◆ Create tiny sensors that will scan the body to seek out infectious agents

Many imaginative uses of nanotechnology in medicine are currently being discussed. For example, cancer specialists someday may have available miniature "nanotools" that will seek out and annihilate cancer cells while they are only starting to develop into a tumor, and thus prevent the disease altogether. Developing nanomedicine tools and techniques may also allow a concentration of drugs to be delivered to selected target tissues, a capability that would likely minimize drug side effects and toxicity. Around the world, many scientists are involved in this new field of study. In years to come, researchers anticipate reaching ever-higher levels of innovations to cure or prevent disease and enhance human health.

RECOMBINANT DNA (rDNA)

Also known as gene splicing or genetic engineering, the rDNA process results in making a new gene. The general process remains controversial; many people worry that these new genes may be unexpectedly dangerous. Interestingly, these societal concerns do not seem to extend to genetically engineered drugs. Many of these are already on the market, including allergy drugs, insulin, and beta-blockers. Beta-blockers block a hormone that increases blood pressure and heart rate. Blocking the hormone then reduces blood pressure and lowers the heart rate to help prevent heart attacks. For some time, patients with CF have been benefiting from the recombinant human drug Pulmozyme, the drug prescribed to improve lung function by thinning mucus that clogs the patient's airways.

At its basic level, combining two or more DNA strands creates an entirely new DNA that has the ability to build a new protein (gene) in a host cell. But before the new protein can be built, rDNA must be present to deliver the instructions for doing so. Scientists use expression vectors to introduce the rDNA into the host cell. The vectors kick-start the protein expression process by emitting signals that instruct the cell's normal function in how to transcribe and translate the new gene.

The promise of rDNA involves research and production of a wide range of rDNA medicines. In addition to preventing and/or curing inherited genetic diseases such as CF, these sophisticated drugs may someday do the same for sickle-cell anemia and many other genetic diseases and medical conditions.

Increasing numbers of rDNA studies are under way in other fields, as well. The genetic engineering process not only holds promise for human health, it is also under development for advancing industrial products and for creating increasingly robust agricultural plants, such as disease-resistant potatoes and other foods.

BUILDING A KNOWLEDGE BASE

There is a snowball effect in developing the promising high-tech solutions for treating or curing cystic fibrosis and other diseases. As a new area of medical research emerges and becomes increasingly recognized by scientists as showing potential for creating novel treatments or cures, the pace of discovery intensifies. More research groups actively begin exploring and developing tools and techniques that help deepen their understanding of disease. Scientific knowledge grows from these many research

STEM CELL RESEARCH

Stem cells are basic, unspecialized cells in human embryos that eventually grow and change into every body cell type, including cells that make organs, tissues, bones, brains, and every other body part (Figure 7.2). The idea of using human embryos to harvest stem cells for research remains highly controversial from ethical, religious, and societal viewpoints.

In 2001, then-President George W. Bush prohibited federal funding for development of new stem cell lines, although he supported research funding for using the 60 stem cell lines that already existed. Researchers continue to work from this existing pool of stem cells to develop therapeutic approaches to CF, as well as therapy and prevention for thousands of other human maladies. As politics change, so may the restricted use of human embryonic stem cells, as evidenced by President Barack Obama's overturning of Bush's regulations in 2009.

The recent construction of a new human embryonic stem cell line (from an existing cell line) that contains the CFTR gene mutations has allowed researchers to use mutated CFTR cell lines for study. Using these embryonic or adult stem cells to renovate damaged lungs or to control the inflammatory and immune reactions in the lungs are all current research projects. Embryonic stem cells can become all cell types in the body, whereas adult stem cells are limited to changing into different cell types of the body tissue where they originate. CF researchers acknowledge that significant barriers must be overcome before this type of gene therapy can be useful. Although vector technology has improved, it has a way to efforts, and new discoveries evolve and develop. Gene therapy, nanotechnology, pharmacogenomics, and the use of recombinant DNA techniques will continue to mature as

go before it can effectively and safely deliver DNA to cells. Problems in narrowly targeting cells must be solved, and sustaining gene expression must become reality. Also, researchers must gain a better understanding of both inflammatory and immune reactions. Despite these barriers, CF patients are hopeful that stem cell research will yield better treatment options and possibly a cure.

Recent studies using a variety of cell populations gleaned from adult bone marrow and from umbilical cord blood have shown that some of these cells navigate to differing body organs, then adhere to and acquire that organ's distinctive characteristics. This may provide another way to conduct stem cell research. Also, new findings show that stem cells can be created from adult cells that line the inside of a mouse's mouth. But using these types of methods to study humans is years away, according to the researchers.

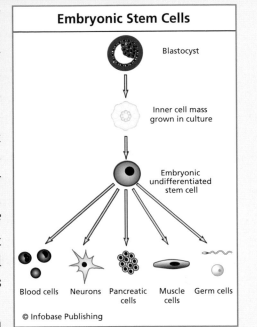

Figure 7.2   Stem cells are unspecialized cells that can develop into any kind of cell.

new knowledge accumulates. These are exciting times for biomedical researchers and for patients with CF and other genetic, chronic medical conditions.

CYSTIC FIBROSIS THERAPIES IN RESEARCH

Developing novel techniques supports the efforts in a variety of experimental treatments for cystic fibrosis. Universities, private companies, federal institutes, and foundations are working toward solving the problems of living with this lethal disease. Much of the current cystic fibrosis research focuses on developing new drugs to treat the most challenging CF problems, including the physical damage from the disease's expression. Drug researchers seek to lessen the effects of CF and improve the use of commonly used drugs. For example, researchers are working to correct the damaged sodium chloride transport function caused by the mutated CFTR protein. Fixing this problem would allow the sodium chloride channel to work properly, which would negate the dehydration that causes the thick mucus and extreme salt loss in CF patients.

8

ETHICAL, SOCIAL, AND LEGAL ISSUES

The exploding area of genetic research and development has already benefited many people. Advances in biology, microbiology, biotechnology, and nanotechnology are now woven throughout the field of medicine. Genetic testing can reveal many abnormalities inside of genes. Testing can disclose whether or not a person carries damaged genes or if an unborn child is at risk for a disease, for example. Working to benefit people is the underlying scientific rationale for exploring and developing innovative treatments and technologies arising from genetic studies. The promising medical benefits of preventing, treating, and possibly curing diseases that have plagued humans for centuries may become reality in the near future.

Although the study of genetics and the development of new treatments holds enormous promise, these studies also raise important ethical, social, and legal issues. The answers to critical questions, such as the morality of working with stem cells, continue to evolve. The range of beliefs spans from full acceptance of all genetic techniques to those who question the ethics and morality of conducting scientific work that uses human genetic matter.

ISSUES SURROUNDING STEM CELL RESEARCH

Using human embryos to harvest stem cells for research remains highly controversial. People around the world continue to discuss the ethical, religious, and political ramifications of the research and methodology. Scientists continue to collect federal funding to support research of the 60 existing diverse stem cell lines. CF researchers are currently using preexisting embryonic stem cell lines and adult stem cells to seek ways to renovate damaged lung cells, as well as to control inflammatory and immune reactions in the lungs. The most recent advance is the development of a cystic fibrosis stem cell line, which offers a large pool of CF DNA material to CF researchers.

GENETICS PERSONALIZED

Many questions about privacy surround individual gene testing. For example:

◆ Who owns a person's genetic profile?
◆ Will a potential employer fairly use a job seeker's highly personal genetic profile?
◆ If a person carries a disease gene, will insurance companies deny coverage if they find out this information?
◆ Will courts having access to personal genetic data lead to the unfair treatment of people with genetic problems?

The answers to these questions are important because the information provided to employers, insurers, school personnel, courts and judges, and other institutions can have a huge impact on a person's livelihood and quality of life.

Gene Testing

Choosing to participate in genetic testing or clinical trials underscores the high stakes that people face when doing so. For example, every person who agrees to serve as the subject of a clinical trial that involves genetic therapy must be fully informed of the risks that are involved.

Potential genetic discrimination by medical personnel, employers, and insurers who have access to a person's genetic profile is a major concern. Increasingly, hospitals are moving into electronic storage of each patient's health and history record. How will this highly private information be handled if it becomes part of an individual's electronic record? Keep in mind that doctors and other health personnel often have easy access to patients' medical records.

Some employers and insurers have already used this personal information to benefit their own situations. Potential employees have been rejected when employers discover that they carry genetic information that could cost the company money in the future. For example, if a woman carries the BRCA1 and/or BRCA2 genes for breast cancer—even though she has not had the disease—these two genes increase a woman's risk of breast cancer during her lifetime. Surgery to remove a breast tumor is costly, as are radiation and drug treatments, and so companies may wish to avoid hiring such women. If the company has access to this kind of genetic information, they could choose to avoid hiring a woman who has tested positive for one or both of these genes. In the late 1990s, the plight of people undergoing preemployment genetic testing came to light when Lawrence Berkeley Laboratory used the practice to discriminate against potential employees. A lawsuit ensued, which found

FIGURE 8.1 Many people seek genetic counseling for information and support concerning genetic diseases they might pass on to their children.

in favor of the employees involved in the 1998 case, *Norman-Bloodsaw v. Lawrence Berkeley Laboratory.*

LEGAL PROTECTION

As yet, no federal laws exist to protect people from all genetic discrimination. However, this gap in protecting human rights was partly filled when Congress passes the Genetic Information Nondiscrimination Act of 2007 (H.R. 493), which provides genetic discrimination protection in employment and in insurance coverage. Both the House and Senate passed amended versions of the act, and on May 21, 2008, President George W. Bush signed the amended bill into law.

Unlike private citizens, federal employees have been protected from workplace discrimination since 2000. They receive health insurance protection from the existing federal law, known as the Federal Employees' Health Benefits Program, which consists of a number of different local, regional, and national heath coverage plans.

Do states legally protect people from genetic discrimination? Some do, but some do not. To date, 41 states have laws that protect people from genetic discrimination by insurance companies. Regarding workplace discrimination, 32 states have laws to protect people. Among those states that do offer some level of protection, the laws are a patchwork of regulations that vary greatly in depth and extent of protection.

GENETIC INJUSTICE

Many years ago, some states passed laws that required the sterilization of people who were suspected of having "genetic defects." Mental retardation, epilepsy, mental illness, blindness, and loss of hearing were all thought to be caused by bad genes. In 1907, the state of Indiana passed the first sterilization law. By as recently as 1981, most states had adopted sterilization laws that were designed to remedy genetic traits or tendencies that were apparent. Many of these state laws have since been repealed or changed to include basic constitutional rights of due process of law and equal protection under the law.

DISCRIMINATION

Discrimination can involve defined populations that carry specific genetic mutations. For example, cystic fibrosis occurs largely in Caucasian groups. On the other hand, sickle-cell anemia is a genetic disease that largely affects African Americans. In the early 1970s, some states pressed forward to pass discriminatory laws that required mandated genetic screening for all African Americans to see if they carried the mutated gene for sickle-cell anemia. Those laws created unnecessary fear and stigmatized the African-American population. In 1972, recognizing the damage that these state laws caused, Congress passed the National Sickle Cell Anemia Control Act. This legislation withholds federal funds from states who have failed to make genetic testing for sickle-cell anemia completely voluntary.

PREGNANCY SCREENING

Prenatal testing is done to discover if either or both parents are CF carriers. The test is performed in a laboratory using a blood or saliva sample. Until recently, prenatal testing was offered mostly to at-risk women; today, it is usually offered to every woman during a routine pregnancy checkup. In increasing numbers, women are finding that carrier screening for CF during pregnancy serves a constructive purpose: Both negative and positive results can help the prospective parents plan for the future. For example, negative test results can give the mother and father a sense of relief that they are likely not CF carriers. (Because some CF mutations are not picked up during screening, people who test negative may still be CF carriers, however.) Conversely, if both partners test positive as carriers, that information gives the couple time to find out for sure if their unborn baby is at high risk for CF. In this case, the doctor may recommend additional tests to determine the baby's CF risk level. Amniocentesis is one such test in which a doctor takes a sample of the amniotic fluid that surrounds the fetus inside the

PROS AND CONS OF GENETIC TESTING

Undergoing genetic testing can lead to both positive and negative outcomes. If CF runs in a family, for example, individual members may wish to have genetic carrier testing done. But the decision to test carries many consequences that may directly affect the individual. Genetic counseling can help people carefully examine and consider all the pros and cons of genetic testing (Figure 8.1). Whatever information and recommendations a person gains from the experts, the choice to be tested is solely the individual's. No one can coerce another person to undergo genetic testing.

mother's uterus. The sample contains chromosomes, genes, and chemicals that can be examined to diagnose whether or not the unborn child has CF.

There are no therapies currently available to treat an unborn child with CF, so if the baby's risk is high, the mother can use that information to make decisions. Should she continue the pregnancy? What type of specialists are available for her and the baby? What educational and counseling services are available to her and her family? Difficult choices lie ahead, and genetic or other health-care counseling can provide vital support and information.

Where can a woman find help in making this decision? How might her decision fit with her religious beliefs and teachings? Expert genetic and other counseling can offer support and a safe place for her to discuss options and make a choice that fits her and her family's needs. A couple can work as a team and gain strength and support as they explore their options and work through the emotional issues they are experiencing.

Speaking In Support

An individual who chooses to have genetic testing done must be clear about why they want the test. What will the individual gain by these tests? One answer may be that a negative result may alleviate worry about the possibility of suffering from a specific illness. A positive result may motivate the individual to make lifestyle changes to reduce risk of developing the disease. Stopping smoking, for example, greatly reduces the risk of lung cancer, which has been found to have a genetic element. Finally, if results are positive, the

WHERE TO FIND HELP

A person's doctor is a prime source for information about resources for both genetic and psychological counseling. Also, professionals who work at genetic testing centers may be good referral sources, as well.

But working with people in the cystic fibrosis field may offer the best help. The Cystic Fibrosis Foundation (www.cff.org) can provide considerable assistance. The group offers a wide variety of services, including information about CF, its genetics, pregnancy and therapy options, and more. The organization was formed to ensure ongoing research and development into the cure and control of CF and to support patients' quality of life. It also helps to fund large CF research projects. Cystic Fibrosis Foundation support groups are active around the country; talking with other parents of CF children can provide insights and support.

The National Institutes of Health offers assistance, too. The NIH funds a Web site titled "U.S. Clinic Directory Search," where online users can locate nationwide genetic testing facilities, counseling services, and risk-assessment organizations. The doctor will know how frequently to examine the individual if and when the particular disease begins to express itself.

Speaking Against

Some people may request testing to find out if they carry disease-causing genes. Yet, knowledge can add burdens as well as many benefits to a person's life. Before becoming a candidate for testing, a person usually discusses the family's history of the specific disease beforehand with his or her doctor. The history helps the doctor determine if the person

Web site is located at www.genetests.org and is sponsored by the University of Washington in Seattle.

Planned Parenthood is a long-standing organization with many branches across the country. This group provides a variety of services, including counseling and assistance in making the decision about continuing a pregnancy or ending it via abortion. If a woman chooses abortion, many branches offer abortion services; if the woman chooses to continue the pregnancy, the organization will refer her to another facility.

If the mother chooses to continue the pregnancy and keep the baby, many issues must be addressed. For example, how will she and her partner cope with providing intensive daily care and repeated visits to the doctor? How will they deal with the many hospitalizations that CF patients usually require? These and other decisions may affect career choices and other changes, as well. Will their insurance pay for expensive medical care? If not, how will they pay for it? Do they need to move closer to better care facilities and hospitals? Many services can help with exploring those options and obtaining counseling.

is at high or low risk for the inherited disease. The doctor can then explore with the individual how test results may or may not be helpful. One important aspect that candidates for genetic testing must know is that such testing is inherently limited in the findings it reveals. Factors contributing to these constraints include:

- Genetic tests often fail to detect all mutations that can cause a disease. For example, the damaged CFTR gene contains more than a thousand mutations, and most of those are rare and undetectable. Also, some inherited diseases involve more than one gene, making testing either difficult or impossible.
- Having a positive result does not predict disease; it just tells the individual that they have a mutation associated with a certain illness. The risk for developing that disease may range from high to low. Also, a positive result cannot predict the severity of an inherited disease.
- A negative result does not rule out all chances that an individual will develop a disease. Erratic, random changes in genes can occur that may cause the person undergoing the testing to develop a noninherited disease. Also, environmental factors can damage genes and trigger cancer. For example, many cancers result from smoking and/or overexposure to sunlight.
- Testing for specific genes is just a small part of solving the many mysteries of disease. Nearly all cancers and problems such as heart disease surface from numerous causes, including harmful interactions between genes.
- Genetic testing is expensive, and ranges in cost from less than $100 to more than $2,000, according

to the Genetic Home Reference, National Library of Medicine, a sector of the NIH.

If someone tests positive as a CF carrier, knowing that he or she carries a damaged gene can impart great emotional stress. Worrying about the possibility of becoming ill sometime in the future, feeling guilty about carrying a mutated gene, and experiencing fear and ambivalence about starting a family are just a few of the heavy emotional burdens that a CF carrier must bear.

NEWBORN SCREENING

Every year 4 million newborns in the United States are routinely tested for genetic disorders, including CF, phenylketonuria (an inborn metabolism error), and other conditions,

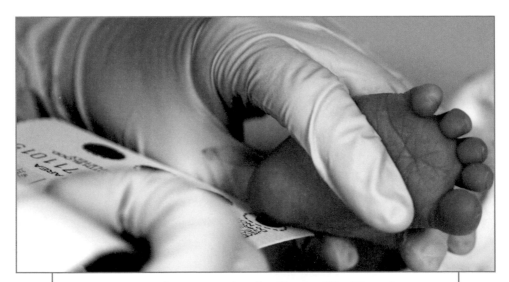

FIGURE 8.2 Newborn screening for diseases like CF are important because many people display no symptoms of the disease but unknowingly carry the gene. Screening typically involves taking a small amount of blood from the heel of an infant that is only a few days old.

according to the National Health Museum. Newborn screening for CF is especially important because more than 10 million Americans have no symptoms but unknowingly carry the CF gene. Yet even if the parents' carrier tests are negative, their baby might still be born with CF. How could that happen? Because carrier testing picks up only the most common mutations of the more than 1,000 mutations that exist in the damaged CFTR gene.

If a newborn is diagnosed with CF, immediate treatment, such as enzyme replacement therapy, prevents much of the damage caused by malnutrition in CF individuals. Adding early nutritional therapies significantly benefits a baby with CF. As they grow, these children show improved height, weight, and critical thinking functions, according to the Cystic Fibrosis Foundation. Early intervention may also improve breathing function, increase life expectancy, and reduce hospitalizations. Already, 36 states require newborn screening, and CF professionals strongly recommend that the rest of the states do the same.

GLOSSARY

Aerosolized medication   Drugs made with suspended solids within a gas that can be inhaled to ease breathing.

Allele   A variant form of a gene located at a specific site on a chromosome.

Amino acid   The basic subunits that form proteins.

Anaerobes   Organisms that do not require oxygen to survive.

Antigen   Any substance capable of triggering an immune response.

Anti-inflammatory medication   Drugs that counteract inflammation.

Aspergillus fumigatus   A fungus that can cause airway inflammation.

Bases   Adenine, guanine, cytosine, thymine (A, G, C, T), and uracil (U)—nucleotides that code hereditary information in the genetic code of DNA and RNA.

Bile   Fluid excreted by the liver that aids in the digestion of fats.

Bowel   A segment of the intestines.

Bowel obstruction   A complete blockage of the intestine from hard stools (feces) that cannot pass through a bowel movement. Bowel obstruction can also occur if one bowel segment slides down inside its contiguous section of bowel. This is called intussusception.

Bronchi   Large air tubes that lead from the throat to the lungs.

Bronchitis   Inflammation of the bronchi.

Bronchodilator   Drugs that expand (dilate) the bronchi to make breathing easier.

Cadaver   A dead human body.

Carbohydrates   Organic compounds such as sugars and starches that are used by cells to store and release energy.

Carrier   A person who carries a gene for a disease but does not have the disease.

Cell   The smallest structural unit of all organisms.

CFTR gene   The cystic fibrosis transmembrane conductance regulator (CFTR) gene is a defective gene that obstructs the normal flow of chloride and fluids in and out of cells.

Chloride channel function   The process of transporting salt and fluid across cellular tissues that line a body tube or that enclose and protect other body parts, among other functions.

Chromosome   A cluster of coiled strands of DNA that contains numerous genes.

Cirrhosis   A hardening of the liver.

Clone   An exact copy of a molecule, cell, or organism.

Codon   A particular sequence of three adjacent nitrogen bases on a strand of DNA or RNA that gives the genetic code for production of a specific amino acid.

Comparative genomics   The study of human genetics through comparison to other living things, such as mice, fruit flies, and rhesus monkeys.

Compound   A substance formed by the union of one or more various chemicals.

Constipation   Delayed or infrequent bowel movements caused by hard, dry feces.

Cytoplasm   The gelatinous substance outside of a cell's nucleus in which the cell's organelles are suspended.

Dehydration   Abnormal reduction of body fluids.

Deoxyribonucleic acid (DNA)   A chemical located primarily in a cell's nucleus that carries genetic information.

Diabetes   Abnormal carbohydrate metabolism based on inadequate secretion or usage of insulin.

Diarrhea   Abnormally frequent bowel movements, usually excreted as fluid-like feces.

Digestive enzymes   Complex proteins necessary for normal digestion of food.

DNA microarray   A research technique that allows scientists to study how a cell normally works and what happens when any of its genes work improperly.

DNA microchip technology   A new way for scientists to identify genetic mutations.

DNA mutation analysis   The study of genetic disease processes.

DNA replication   Copying a DNA molecule.

DNA sequencing   A process for finding out the precise order of the base pairs in a piece of DNA.

Double helix   The twisted-ladder form that two strands of DNA take on when their complementary nucleotides bond together.

Electrode   A conductor that is used to establish electrical contact with a nonmetallic substance.

Embryo   The earliest stage of growth and development; in humans, the stage spans from fertilization up to nine weeks' gestation.

Endoscope   A tool for seeing inside a hollow organ.

Fats   A type of organic compound made from fatty acids that contain a high caloric (or energy) value. Butter and olive oil are two of the many foods made from types of fats.

Fat-soluble vitamins   Essential nutrients (vitamins A, D, E, and K) stored in the liver and fatty tissue.

Fertilization   The union of male and female reproductive sex cells.

Fluorescence in situ hybridization (FISH)   A technique used to envision and map genetic substances in a person's cells.

Fluorescent dye   Used in varying colors, these dyes identify the probes that researchers use to discover exactly where a specific gene sits inside a person's chromosomes.

Gene   The working physical unit of heredity that passes from parent to child.

Gene expression   Completion of the entire process of building proteins encoded in DNA.

Gene sequencing   The process by which the order of nucleotides in a gene is determined.

Gene therapy   An experimental technique aiming to treat inherited diseases by replacing, manipulating, or supplementing damaged genes with healthy ones.

Genetic code   Specific codes stored in each strand of DNA and RNA for building specific proteins.

Genetic marker   A piece of DNA in which the physical location on a chromosome can be identified and used to follow inheritance.

Genetics   A branch of biology that works with heredity and variations of organisms, including humans.

Genome-wide association studies   Here, researchers use new tools and technologies to swiftly analyze genetic differences between individuals with particular illnesses (heart disease and diabetes, for example) as compared to the genetic makeup of healthy people.

Genotyping   The process of finding out the genotype of an individual.

Globular   Having the shape of a globe.

Glucose intolerant   Having a decreased ability to metabolize sugar adequately.

HapMap   An international effort to identify and catalog all genetic similarities and differences among people.

Hippocrates   A Greek physician, regarded as the founder of medicine.

Hormone   An internal substance that triggers a stimulatory effect on cellular activity.

Human Genome Project (HGP)   An international research initiative to sequence and map all human genes in the human genome. Completed in 2003, the project allowed scientists a way to visualize the complete genetic design plan for building a human being.

Infertility   The inability to become pregnant, or in men, the inability to father a child.

Inherited   A trait that is passed from parent to child.

Insulin   A pancreatic hormone that is necessary for metabolism of carbohydrates.

Intravenous   Administration of a drug or fluid into a vein.

Knockout mouse   A research mouse in which researchers inactivate (or knock out) an existing gene by using an artificial piece of DNA to replace it or disrupt its activity.

Ligament   A tough band of tissue that links bones to one another and hold organs in place.

Linkage study   A study that seeks to establish linkage between genes, which occurs because of their location near each other on the same chromosome.

Liposomes   Fatty droplets in a cell's cytoplasm.

Mapping   Gene mapping aiming to discover the relative positions of genes on a chromosome or piece of DNA.

Meconium   The dark, greenish mass of cells, mucus, and bile that accumulates in a fetus's bowel and is discharged soon after birth.

Metabolic   Producing energy for body processes and activities from chemical changes in body cells.

Model organisms   Nonhuman life forms, such as mice, that provide strong data sets to compare to the human genome.

Molecular biology   The study of living material on a molecular level that examines the structure, function, and composition of important molecules such as DNA and RNA.

Molecule   The smallest unit of a compound; two or more atoms chemically combined.

Mutation   A change in a sequence of DNA or RNA.

Nanomedicine   A medical and pharmaceutical science in which researchers work on a nanometer scale (one billionth of a meter).

Nanotechnology   The broad area in science that comprises nanomedicine and other technical fields. Scientists create and use ingredients and devices as small as molecules and atoms in their research.

Nasal polyp   A long outgrowth of tissue in the lining of the nose.

Nuclear envelope   The double membrane that encloses a cell's nucleus.

Nucleotide   A building block of DNA that is composed of one of four nitrogen bases: adenine, guanine, thymine, and cystosine, along with a molecule of sugar and a molecule of phosphoric acid.

Nucleus   The structure inside of a cell that controls most cell functions and contains genetic material.

Operator genes Genes that trigger the production of messenger RNA through adjacent structural genes.

Oral glucose tolerance test A series of blood tests performed at certain intervals to increase an individual's glucose (i.e., blood sugar) intake and track his or her blood glucose levels over time. The test is often used to help diagnose diabetes.

Organ transplantation Surgical replacement of a poorly operating human organ with a healthy one.

Pancreas A large gland that secretes digestive enzymes and produces insulin.

Pharmacogenomics A science that studies inherent genetic differences that determine a person's response to a drug.

Phenotype Observable traits in a living thing.

Phlegm An overabundance of mucus secreted in the respiratory tract.

Plasma The fluid part of blood.

Pneumonia A disease of inflammation and infection in the lungs.

Polymerase chain reaction A common method of creating copies of specific segments of DNA.

Polymorphisms Differing forms of an organism that the organism itself produces.

Positional cloning A process that uses gene mapping techniques to locate a gene responsible for a disease when little or no information about the biochemical foundation of the disease is known.

Postural drainage Several techniques for loosening thick mucus from the lungs and airways so that the patient can cough the mucus out to breathe easier.

Prenatal The period of time before birth.

Prokaryotic cells   Cells such as bacteria in which the genetic material is not contained in a nuclear envelope and that lack other membrane-bound organelles.

Proteins   Molecules made from groups of amino acids; they are necessary for body structure and function.

Pseudomonas aeruginosa   A bacterium that opportunistically infects people with poorly functioning immune systems. It colonizes in the lungs of CF patients and can cause serious damage.

Recessive gene   A gene that produces its individual phenotype only if its allele is identical. For example, cystic fibrosis is passed on to a child only if both parents contribute their recessive copies of the CFTR gene during fertilization.

Recombinant DNA (rDNA)   A new DNA sequence artificially produced by connecting pieces of DNA from different organisms.

Replacement enzymes   CF patients often take these enzymes to replace the pancreatic enzymes that they lack to aid in digestion.

Restriction enzymes   Enzymes that recognize very precise areas of a DNA sequence, then cut it at those points. This step is part of the cloning process.

Ribonucleic acid (RNA)   RNA acts as a messenger between DNA and ribosomes. RNA also makes proteins from amino acids. It is single stranded and contains the nitrogen base uracil instead of thymine.

Ribosome   A miniscule particle made of RNA and protein that is located in the cytoplasm of living cells. It is the site for building the polypeptides encoded by mRNA.

Semen   A viscous fluid of the male reproductive organs that carries the sperm outside of the body.

Sinus   A cavity or hollow area in the body.

Sinusitis   An inflammation of the sinuses.

Sodium chloride   A molecule made up of an atom of sodium and an atom of chlorine, held together by an ionic bond; salt.

Sputum   Saliva material that is spit out.

Steroid medications   A class of potent prescription drugs used to treat loss of lean muscle mass and to lessen lung inflammation in individuals with CF and asthma, among many other anti-inflammatory uses.

Stools   Solid waste that is passed through bowel movements.

Transcription   A process in the cell nucleus in which an RNA copy is made of a DNA strand.

Transcriptome   A compilation of all gene transcripts in a given cell, which will be transcribed into messenger RNA (mRNA) and transport the genetic instructions to the cell's ribosomes for initiating protein production.

Translation   The step that converts the information in an RNA sequence into a sequence of amino acids, which link together to form a protein.

Trypsinogen   The early form of trypsin, a pancreatic enzyme.

Vas deferens   The tube that joins with the seminal vesicle to form the duct through which a man's semen will pass to the outside of the body. Often called the sperm duct.

Vector   A form of gene delivery to a specific site in the body.

Voltage measurements   Measurements of a unit of electricity (volts). Voltage measurements are taken across the lining of the nose to help make the diagnosis of CF.

BIBLIOGRAPHY

Accurso, F. "Update in Cystic Fibrosis 2006." *American Journal of Respiratory Critical Care Medicine* 175 (April 16, 2007): 754–57.

Haber, H. "Cystic Fibrosis in Children and Young Adults: Findings on Routine Abdominal Sonography." *American Journal of Roentgenology* 189 (July 2007): 89–99.

Hadjiliadis, D. "Special Considerations for Patients With Cystic Fibrosis Undergoing Lung Transplantation." *Chest* 131 (April 2007): 1224–31.

Harris, A. and M. Super. *Cystic Fibrosis: The Facts*. New York: Oxford University Press, 1995.

Hodson, M., D. Geddes, W. Tranquilli, K. Grimm, and L. Lamont. *Cystic Fibrosis*. New York, NY: Oxford University Press, 2000.

Kepron, Wayne. *Cystic Fibrosis: Surviving Childhood, Achieving Adulthood (Your Personal Health)*. Buffalo, N.Y.: Firefly Books, 2004.

LeGrys, V., J. Yankaskas, L. Quittell, B. Marshall, and P. Mogayzel. "Diagnostic Sweat Testing: The Cystic Fibrosis Foundation Guidelines." *Journal of Pediatrics* 151 (July 2007): 85–89.

Public Broadcasting System. "Cracking the Code of Life." *NOVA*. Available online: http://www.pbs.org/wgbh/nova/genome/deco_collins.html.

Riordan, J., J. Rommens, B. Kerem, et al. "Identification of the Cystic Fibrosis Gene: Cloning and Characterization of

Complementary DNA." *Science* 245 (September 8, 1989): 1066–73.

Serisier, D., A. Coates, and S. Bowler. "Effect of Albuterol on Maximal Exercise Capacity in Cystic Fibrosis." *Chest* 131 (April 2007): 1181–87.

Shepherd, R., and G. Cleghorn. *Cystic Fibrosis: Nutritional and Intestinal Disorders.* Boca Raton, Fla.: CRC Press, 1989.

Welsh, M. and R. Fick, "Cystic Fibrosis." *Journal of Clinical Investigation* 80 (December 1987): 1523–26.

Wicks E., "Cystic Fibrosis." *British Medical Journal* 334 (June 16, 2007): 1231–32.

FURTHER RESOURCES

Apel, Melanie Ann. *Cystic Fibrosis: The Ultimate Teen Guide (It Happened to Me)*. Lanham, Md.: Scarecrow Press, 2006.

Byrnes, Isabel Stenzel, and Anabel Stenzel. *The Power of Two: A Twin Triumph Over Cystic Fibrosis*. Columbia, Miss.: University of Missouri Press, 2007.

Deford, Frank. *Alex: The Life of a Child*. Nashville, Tenn.: Thomas Nelson Publisher, 1997.

Henry, Cynthia S. *Taking Cystic Fibrosis to School*. Plainville, N.Y.: JayJo Books, 2000.

Lux, Carrie. *Little Brave Ones: For Children Who Battle Cystic Fibrosis*. Charleston, S.C.: BookSurge Publishing, 2006.

Mullin, Teresa Anne. *The Stones Applaud: How Cystic Fibrosis Shaped My Childhood*. Franklin, Tenn.: Providence House Publishers, 2007.

Peebles, Allison, Gary J. Connett, Judi C. Maddison, and Joan Gavin. *Cystic Fibrosis Care: A Practical Guide*. Philadelphia: Churchill Livingstone, 2005.

Wailoo, Keith, and Stephen Pemberton. *The Troubled Dream of Genetic Medicine: Ethnicity and Innovation in Tay-Sachs, Cystic Fibrosis, and Sickle Cell Disease*. Baltimore, Md.: Johns Hopkins University Press, 2006.

WEB SITES
Cystic Fibrosis Center at Stanford University
http://cfcenter.stanford.edu/
A joint venture between the Stanford University Hospital and Lucille Packard Children's Hospital, the Cystic Fibrosis Center

conducts research on CF treatments and provides medical and social services to CF patients and their families.

Cystic Fibrosis Foundation
http://www.cff.org
The nonprofit Cystic Fibrosis Foundation is dedicated to funding medical research for new therapies to help those living with CF.

Cystic Fibrosis: Diet and Nutrition
http://kidshealth.org/kid/nutrition/diets/cf_diet.html
Featuring recipes and a brief explanation of CF, this Web site is a nutritional guide for children and teens with the disease.

Cystic Fibrosis: Your Genes, Your Health
http://www.yourgenesyourhealth.org/cf/whatisit.htm
Created by the Dolan DNA Learning Center, this Web site uses interactive graphics to explain the causes, symptoms, and treatments of CF.

National Human Genome Research Institute
http://www.genome.gov
As part of the National Institutes of Health, the National Human Genome Research Institute began as a research center focused on mapping the human genome. Their Web site provides an in-depth explanation of the Human Genome Project and brief history of genomics.

Office of Rare Diseases Research (National Institutes of Health)
http://rarediseases.info.nih.gov/
A portal Web site created by the Office of Rare Diseases Research designed to assist those who seek information and support on diseases like CF.

PICTURE CREDITS

INDEX

ABOUT THE AUTHOR

Sharon Giddings is a registered nurse who holds a Bachelor of Science degree in nursing from Michigan State University. She also has received a master's degree in journalism from the University of Missouri at Columbia. For more than 18 years, her work has appeared nationally and internationally in newspapers, magazines, on the web, and in other printed media. She has been a managing editor of a global monthly clinical trials magazine and currently serves as a contributing editor and editorial judge for a nationally circulated radiology and imaging trade magazine and others published by its parent company. She has written for various publications throughout the National Institutes of Health and has reported on health care reform issues from the U.S. Capitol. Ms. Giddings lives with her husband on their timber ranch in the lush, green Oregon mountains. Her special interest is to write about medical conditions and genetic issues that affect both children and adults.